BLACKBERRIES IN JULY

A FORAGER'S FIELD GUIDE TO INNER PEACE

Tom A. Titus

Cover art and illustration by Kristine A. Kirkeby

First Printing

A Red Moons Press Publication

ISBN-13: 978-0-9847324-5-6
ISBN-10: 0-9847324-5-4

For my wife Kim,
loving keeper of
my words and
my world.

CONTENTS

THANK YOU

When I began this first book, the depth of my naïveté was astonishing. Much of my innocence came from thinking that writing is a solitary exercise. Never could I have anticipated the number of friends and family who imparted their raven wisdom and along the way contributed mightily to my writing and the interconnectedness of my personal ecology. All will have my gratitude until that last sighing breath carries me on to whatever is next.

Kim Wollter was my copy editor, design engineer, literary critic, curator of recent family history, and long-suffering therapist who listened while I complained, unreasonably compared myself to others, and on many occasions swore to quit this project. The book you hold would not exist without her constant encouragement and careful attention to detail on every level. Perhaps I would not exist either.

Tom and Barbara Titus are, after more than five decades, still raising me with a wise combination of love and wild freedom. They shared their memories of family members long passed and were valuable critics of early versions of the manuscript.

Red Moons, my critique group, has been my critical cheerleading section for more years than I now care to count. Cliff Scovell was the first among us to travel the twisting path toward digital publishing, and he was instrumental in formatting the final manuscript. Thanks especially to Jessica Maxwell, patient persistent Red Moons Mother Hen, Scottish red-headed fire and vapor, see-er of books in people like me who never could have seen one for themselves, and without whom I would not have started nor finished this project.

Kris Kirkeby wandered boldly into the tangled shadows of my imagination and returned with sunlit blackberries artfully arranged in a beautiful book cover.

Many friends read and critiqued various pieces and versions of this manuscript: Dan Armstrong, John Carter, Melody Clarkson, Cara DiMarco, Jerry Gatchell, Martha Gatchell, Charles Goodrich, Ellen McCumsey, Judy Osgood, Ken Shindledecker, Holly Simons, Cathy Ward, and Charlie Ward. They know me well and will not be surprised when I didn't always follow their advice. Please understand that I took all of their remarks seriously.

TAT
June 2012

PREFACE

I love living things—that is the nature of biologists. I love living books, too, and I suppose that is the nature of writers. What fascinates me about living things and living books is that neither have clear beginnings or endings. I can't pinpoint the place in time when *Blackberries in July* began any more than anyone can establish that magical moment when a life begins, because all beginnings that ever were can be subdivided into slices of time that become thinner and thinner, smaller and smaller, so that the harder we look the more they eventually blur into a continuum with no clear boundaries. Nevertheless, I'm going to point my pointer finger and at least waggle it in the general direction of a beginning.

This book about coming home to Oregon was born on a plane headed for southern California. My family and I had settled in for a trip to Disneyland when I spotted the deep red curls a few seats in front of me that could only have been the back of author Jessica Maxwell's head. Jessica and I met several years before when she and her namesake nephew Jesse accompanied me on a field trip looking for salamanders in the Oregon Coast Range. At the end of the day she had promised me a Key Lime pie, which I had never collected, and I decided to reacquaint myself. We spent the flight talking about life and her idea for a new adventure travel book. The jet was leveling off for the final leg into the smoggy Los Angeles Basin when Jessica looked at me unflinchingly.

"Do you have a book in you?"

1

The plane drifted down. I had a funny feeling in my stomach.

"I dunno, how about this?" I ventured.

A young fourth generation Oregonian moves to the Midwest because someone said that he had to do this for the sake of his career. He is homesick because he grew up around rivers with trout and mountains with elk and valleys with geese. He misses the bounded freedom of his traditions and people who are like him and those who are not like him but care about him anyway. He tries to fill that void by devouring his new career and becomes pretty good at what he does. But always there is that unsatisfied, unfilled space. That hole. Ten years later he and his young family return home on vacation at the harvest end of a summer shrugging into September, when the nights begin cooling and trout are fat and elk are bugling and the grass is brown and the family pasture sends the green sweet smell of borage and pennyroyal swirling into moist morning air. The man and his family go back to that work a long way from home. The hole gapes open. It hurts. For some reason the Universe doesn't like holes, especially holes in people, and events driven by intention conspire to bring the man and his family back to Oregon for good. He begins a new life that becomes the old ways of the land: digging clams on smelly black mudflats, beekeeping in white apple blossom spring, gathering summer blackberries, manic fall salmon fishing, and cider pressing in old family orchards. But he also needs to figure out how to move away from the well-blazed trail of his career and still pay the bills. This turns out to be really hard, harder than he ever anticipated. Yet in the end it all works out well, and the hole is filled.

Jessica thought this would make a pretty good book. I decided she was right. So I set about describing a year in my life—stories about the things that I do over the progression of seasons that anchor me to my place and my people in the Northwest. The stories are arranged in a chronological year, beginning in the soaking wet bud swell of late winter and finishing in the salmon dying darkness and rebirth of the December Solstice. The particulars actually take place over many seasons of many years, and the wisdom that took root also grew over all those years, often from the introspection of writing. Everything has been compressed in time to capture the seasonal flow and personal transformation that came from living and really *being* in this place. All coalesces into one really dynamic year.

Thomas Wolfe said "you can't go home again." I did it anyway. Come walk with me and I'll show you why.

Blackberries in July

LATE WINTER RAIN

At times I'm an insect
dangling in a web,
outside shiny and intact,
inside sucked dry,
an unwilling liar.

That bug fed a spider but
I don't remember feeding anyone.
Or maybe I did and
along the way
forgot to eat.

I've seen some things—
stood on a dark ridge
holding Night as she labored,
orange dawn oozing across dim sky,
pushing a red crown over
distant hills.

Drank infant water
seeping quietly into light,
dribbling unintelligibly
beneath mossy stones,
chattering downhill

to find kin in
a twisting canyon,
becoming one forceful river
self-assured.

I'm not blind. Really.
These are the many
faces of Spirit.
Yet sometimes
when I'm empty
I wonder where
Joy begins.

I'm a blue collar Ph.D., a bow-hunting conservationist, a bird-watching duck hunter, a traditionalist scrambling to keep up with the times, an evolutionary biologist who believes in human consciousness. I have family and friends I would die for but am often happiest when I'm alone. I'm a writhing tangle of contradictions, a roiling kettle of points and counterpoints, a stormy sea of internal debate. Yet at one point in my life I managed to wade into the center of this emotional spiritual intellectual maelstrom and emerge with a purpose for my life: to experience deep inner peace. No problem.

To me, the idea of an internal state of serenity still seems pretty far-fetched, but I've learned a few things. One of those things is that my existence is like an ongoing chemical reaction; it precipitates a lot of stuff, and the bits and pieces need to settle out occasionally. So I set aside some time every February, my birthday month, to sift through this flotsam, passing the odds and ends through the sieve of consciousness, holding them up to the light, inspecting each one for some previously hidden glimmer, something that might justify the space they occupy in memory.

This morning I drive a meandering road deep into the Oregon Coast Range, where wet wrinkly ridges, narrow watery canyons, and evergreen forest are scrunched between the blue-gray vastness of the Pacific Ocean and the flat green farmlands of the Willamette Valley, a place where nine months of rain drive birth and death and growth and decay and rebirth at such a frenetic pace that all flow into a peaceful drippy singularity. Everything here either is or once was in a fluid state. Even the core of these mountains is cold seafloor pressed into beige sandstone that was riddled with red hot flows of liquid basalt that now stand stalwart and gray. Some of the mountains were lonely drifting islands in the Pacific that fell into the embrace of the North American plate as it advanced on its tectonic journey westward. The Coast Range has a 60-million-year lifetime of scars, incised by the gentle but relentless action of water that falls on pointed needles and round leaves and soft moss and hard rock and collects into streams twisting through tight canyon bottoms like tannin-colored snakes carrying the sandstone back to the sea.

Other wounds are recent. After one and a half centuries of ongoing logging, most hillsides have been cut and are in various stages of healing, crisscrossed by roads and red-dirt landslides. A few small places have been spared the saws. These are secret refuges for reflection, quiet spaces for contemplation. Parking the pickup, I stand at the mouth of one such canyon, inspecting the trail inward. Steep hillsides of dark green Douglas fir are

7

interspersed by groves of red alder adorned only with maroon catkins. The sharp contours of ridges and treetops soften under pockets of fog settling in the draws like gray goose down. Moisture seeps from every pore of the mountains, trickling downhill in rivulets of cold sweat that converge in a small creek gurgling out of the canyon, iced-tea water slipping softly past naked willows. Late winter rain drips gently from leafless limbs and evergreen boughs, murmuring an accompaniment to the whispering stream, coalescing in a quiet symphony of water directed by gravity, falling then dribbling then flowing over the face of the land.

An old logging road enters the gap in the mountains on the east side, the conduit by which the trees near the canyon mouth were removed. The surrounding slopes are covered with fifteen-year-old fir, and the narrow valley floor is a nearly impervious snarl of maples, cascara, red alder, and blackberry brambles that are rapidly reclaiming the road and transforming it into an overgrown trail. Deer have used it, ducking under the overhanging brambles. The animals know best how to negotiate the steep terrain and dense vegetation, and I follow their lead, walking slowly and carefully, swishing against wet brush along the narrow path and cussing an overly aggressive blackberry vine that grabs at my hat. Rough-skinned newts with cocoa backs and tangerine bellies lie motionless in a pair of water-filled ruts made by some misguided traveler who thought this unkempt track would take them somewhere. By vehicle the road goes nowhere. But on foot the possibilities are limitless, and this morning the path becomes a wandering deliberation on life.

When I finished my Ph.D. I had three seconds of elation. These came two days after the party, when I was on my way to the hardware store. Joy broke like a bright moth from the hard chrysalis of my chest, flitting quickly away, disappearing over the gray January horizon of eastern Kansas. I'd worked my butt off for that degree, and in my rear view mirror was seven years of living a long way from home and working more 70-hour weeks at a starvation salary than most workaday overtime junkies could even dream of. I had stretched, grown, proven myself in the fires of the academic furnace, managed to get and stay married, and somehow found time to start raising two kids while filling my resume with all the right stuff: awards, grants, research papers, and references from good people who would go to bat for me in a very competitive field. All of this for three seconds of glory.

Now I was buying wire so that Dad, who had come for graduation and to help us move, could fix the lights on the homemade utility trailer he had built when I was twelve and had given to me as a going-away present when I left Oregon seven years ago. We needed lights on the trailer to move from the Heartland to Long Island and the State University of New York at Stony Brook, the next whistle stop on my academic fast track. This was a postdoctoral position, a period of scholarly transiency and intellectual apprenticeship that would hopefully lead to an academic position somewhere, someday.

After a five-month stint on Long Island we moved on to Washington University in St. Louis for another postdoc position. During our second fall in St. Louis a job was advertised at the University of Colorado, my

perfect job, the job that had seemingly been written using my resume as a template. I remember waving a
sealed envelope containing my application, boldly an-
nouncing to my wife Kim that they would interview me
for this position. The interview came, but autumn became winter and February passed with no decision. My
spirit was prairie flat, worn down, washed out by the St.
Louis winter. I was tired of waiting; waiting on the decision, waiting on spring, waiting on life, waiting on joy. A
crack was forming in my career resolve.

But cracks are where complexity begins; they hold
moisture and become places where moss takes hold and
life starts to reclaim the nonliving. Warm winter rain fell
from a March sky as monotonously gray as the parking
lot was black. My three-year-old daughter Laurel and I
were walking hand-in-hand across this vast expanse of
brooding asphalt behind our rental house when an odor
of rotting leaves rode in on the wet air, stealing into my
nostrils, opening a room somewhere deep in my consciousness that had been locked for a very long time. It
was the smell of chorus frogs trilling in a dying Oregon
winter. A jolt of energy rippled down my spine, crackling
across my psychological overcast, and a clarity rose up
from some deep-down space beyond thought. I knew
immediately that we would return to Oregon.

Without a word from me, Laurel looked up with
large, dark chocolate eyes. "What Dad?"

"Everything's going to be okay," I replied.

And everything was okay. Colorado said "close call,
but no." The University of Oregon said, "bring your
own grant money and we'll make space." So in the heat
and humidity of late summer, Kim gratefully drove west
with Alex and Laurel, revisiting the Grapes of Wrath by

pulling a load of our belongings in that same old utility trailer with the Kansas wiring job behind a 1972 Plymouth Valiant with no air conditioning. I stayed behind to tie up loose ends at work, pack the rest of our rental house, and prepare it for its funeral; our neighborhood was to become a shopping center. A graduate student whose parents lived in Oregon helped me drive a moving truck nonstop across half a continent, locked in the cab with a thermos of coffee that never emptied and our incontinent tabby cat that emptied constantly. Two days later, reeking of cat pee, dazed from too much caffeine and too little sleep, we rolled into the parking area below Mom and Dad's, the house I grew up in. My family walked down the gravel driveway to greet us.

Our return to Oregon started well. We unloaded our belongings into a small house in a tightly knit neighborhood an easy bike ride from work. I paid my own salary from a research grant that would run four more years. By early September we had nearly finished moving in and were planning to hang all the pictures the coming Saturday. But that morning, Mom invited us to pick blueberries with her friend Ethel, who was closing her commercial farm for the season and pulling off the bird netting. You can hang pictures anytime, but the end of blueberry season is here and now. The rest of fall devolved into an unplanned riot of canning, apple picking, trout fishing, and hunting that culminated in an extended family Thanksgiving dinner, our first one in ten years. We hung our pictures in January.

We were very happy. In early summer we went strawberry picking and ate dinner once a week at Mom and Dad's, and on those just-so evenings in June I left the table to fish the same flat slick of river below the home place that I had fished in high school, accompanied by a full moon climbing large and luminous over eastern hills and sulfur yellow duns rising and fluttering above darkening water in the very last light of evening. I took my kids fishing in places I knew they would catch trout. In fall, we picked huckleberries and I hunted deer with the rifle Great Uncle Johnny had sold to me for fifty bucks when I was twelve, the rifle that first belonged to Great Uncle Francis who died in his sleep in his one-room cabin on the hill above Johnny's place. We canned peaches and pears.

But beneath the surface of all this happiness and good fortune something was skulking, a shadowy dark thing that grew slowly over several years. When it rose from the depths and its mouth gaped open, I began to discover that real healing requires more than just family and foraging. The adrenaline surge from my once accelerating career began to subside. Colleagues scratched their heads, and the ghosts of their unfulfilled expectations haunted me. Our money dried up, but the bills flowed in. Eventually the emotional ridges became too steep to climb. Exhausted, I hunkered for most of a year in the foggy bottom of a spiritless canyon.

Healing began when I stopped struggling and was sucked to the very bottom of that black whirlpool. Then I pushed off with both legs toward the surface and into the growing light of February, threw away the Prozac, and walked into the forest where the first tiny blooms of yellow wood violets and pearly white grouse flowers were emerging.

Years later I am still walking. Every February I hike into this steep wet crease of canyon, moving with my feet and traveling into my head, backward and forward and upward and downward and around and through the complex folds of mindfulness. Far inside the narrow valley a deer trail I've been following wriggles through brush and debris scattered across the lower end of a recent clearcut while steady rain freefalls from a battleship sky, unchecked, unabated, uninterrupted, straight to the unprotected ground.

From this open clearcut I step into the waiting arms of a very old forest, and the energy changes abruptly. Frantic regeneration of the logged-over hillside is replaced by quiet stillness. A high canopy of fir boughs filters the rain and mixes it with gray light, spreading both across the understory in a wet film of tarnished silver. Dark evergreen trunks, many of them six feet across, rise from the floor and walls of the canyon, holding the creek in the guarded embrace of sentinels. Logs in various stages of decay lie everywhere. They are sprawled at every angle on the forest floor where their rotting corpses are becoming food for baby hemlock, huckleberry, and salal. They have fallen across the stream, where they catch gravel that right now holds the fertile eggs of Coho salmon that spawned and died here last December. The old forest feels like the quiet wisdom of age. This is the energy of ecological climax.

I close my eyes and see two hundred years behind me, when a rare late summer thunderstorm lit a fire that scorched the canyon, a day when huge fir and red cedar stood tall against the heat until they could take no more and then suddenly erupted in plumes of orange flame and black smoke that sent deer and elk fleeing over the adjoining ridges and salamanders deeper underground. After the ground cooled, gray ash and black charcoal were fertilizer for grasses and annual plants that grew and deflected sunlight and held moisture and died, enriching the soil with organic material. The wettest hillsides sprouted new alder with thin green bark that aged to silver gray like the face of an old blacktail buck. Maple and fir seedlings took hold in drier places. When wet winter storms blew through, fire-blackened snags toppled with an occasional BOOM. Elk and deer returned to the rich new browse and birthed healthy fawns, bears tore open the fallen snags searching for grubs, and a few humans foraged for blackberries and blackcap raspberries under July sun. Trees grew tall again, and sunny hillsides became dancing moisture-laden shade, causing the sun-loving plants and animals to die or move on. Today the rain is falling on the endpoint of this transformational process, an ancient forest woven into an intricate network of sustainable relationships. The forest is complex, stable, and tremendously cohesive.

Leaving the trail, I pick my way down to the creek, jump across an especially narrow riffle, choosing my own way across the canyon bottom, stepping carefully through softly glistening greens of the understory, so many greens that they overflow my brain and spill into a pool deep in my chest, somewhere near my heart. Fresh clover-shaped oxalis is emerging from the moss, and I pick a leaf, chew gently, and let the sour juice seep slowly over the inside of my mouth. A rainy breeze leans against the branches of the overstory with a deep-throated sigh.

Soon I bisect another old roadbed and turn right, moving more deeply into the canyon. From a small marsh to my left, blades of skunk cabbage rise like green canoe paddles and a few early breeding chorus frogs *kree-ick* from the shallow standing water. Farther on, the path crosses a tiny tributary creek that has carved a steep-sided draw. A narrow log spans the creek running ten feet below. I cross on the log, choosing risk, balance, and self-trust over the cumbersome safety of sliding down the bank, wading the creek, and climbing up the other side.

In the watery green womb of this canyon, no judgments are handed down. All of the could-haves should-haves would-haves might-haves if-onlys and victimhood fall away. There is only the dispassionate interwoven nest of the present, a safe place from which to look backward in time. I will not live in the past. But a rear-view glance does provide a point of reference, a sense of direction, a chance for learning, an opportunity for wisdom. Never will I completely understand why choosing the stable ecology of home in Oregon over the successional challenges of my career ambition caused me to shut down, to temporarily lose the complexity of human expression and retreat into an emotionally unstable scorched-earth world. Certainly when we hang all of the weight of our well-being on a single strand—our career, or kids, or material belongings—life can become extremely tenuous and unstable. But I'm a fourth generation Oregonian and was in the process of gathering together the many threads of my place, ready to twist them into an unbreakable cord. This should have been easy.

Perhaps I was trying to straddle two worlds, unsure about committing to another life, even one that was in many ways my old life. This is understandable; I love science, the giddy hits of adrenalin that come with intense learning, teaching, and living under the scrutiny of smart people. I am addicted to discovery. How can I describe the feeling of being the first to see something, even something as outwardly mundane as a brand new DNA sequence from a little known animal? Piecing together these small, daily bits of discovery into larger pictures of understanding is like intellectual crack, and I see why naturalists like Darwin forsook family and home and sailed the world in search of knowledge. But Darwin returned home. I needed to come home also, to begin replacing that heady habit-forming state of being with a new community of thoughts and emotions.

Maybe the only way to move ahead was to first take an ass-over-teakettle tumble into that canyon of emotionless despair, so that when I landed I could finally begin looking upward into the rain, letting it wash away my ego and expectations. Because finally, in that free-falling place of giving up, the scientist in me could entertain a little magic; I found the job that would keep me in biology and keep me in Oregon, where I could buy a small house and raise my kids and visit my mom and dad and pay the bills and spend a rainy day in February walking in an old forest musing on how it all came to pass. I have not thought deeply, nor do I have any strong convictions about illusory things like destiny or fate. But I know that I am lucky, charmed, fortunate, blessed beyond words, and grateful that I was finally able to assemble all of those pieces of living that were there when I stumbled—my family and friends and rain and big trees and blackberries and salmon and wild mushrooms and a wife who shoos me out the door when I need to be alone—into something stable, cohesive, complex, and whole. These are the things that will ensure that I walk into the future in grace.

I belong here.

Ahead, the dim half-light of the high canopy begins to lighten, and before long I am standing hesitantly on the edge of the ancient forest, looking further into the canyon to another clearcut covered with ten-year-old trees. Today I will go no further; the frenetic phase of my life is over. My pants are soaked to the top of my thighs, and I've been moving too slowly to generate enough body heat to fend off a damp chill creeping up my backside. Shivering, I turn back into the protective arms of the old growth, back over the trail home. This is where Joy begins.

OLD ORCHARDS

The rain has stopped. After four wet months of Pacific Northwest darkness I still don't miss Midwestern winters, with brown grass and skeleton trees blowing against skies of frozen blue crystal. Here in the Oregon Coast Range a late winter morning holds the mountains gently, soft overcast wrapping over conifer ridges like the wet mouth of a mother gray fox moving her kits. Smith River Road drops me lightly into a nest of diffuse light and dampness on the forested valley floor, where every bit of ground is covered by growing plants, undaunted by the dimness of winter. Between straight brown shafts of Douglas fir, vine maple eke out an existence in the perennial shade, twisted trunks as green and hard as jade, softened by velvety moss trousers. Sword fern, broad and flat with serrated edges, scatter about in droopy clumps as though the quiet has diffused their taste for combat. They remind me that I am done fighting, too.

Exiting the forest, the road makes a sweeping arc through a meadow containing the Gatchell place. Beneath the leafless walnut tree in front of the old house lies an improvised deck made with plywood and cinder blocks and roofed with a piece of clear plastic. A pair of metal lawn chairs bookend a cable spool tipped on its side to serve as a table for wine glasses and candles and local artifacts—gray lichen, green salal leaves, brown grouse feathers, orange cup fungi. Facing the deck is a conical, outdoor fire pit with a stack of dry fir limbs piled neatly on one side.

Here, in the evenings when those stacked limbs snap into yellow flame, I have become friends with Jerry and Martha. Warming our backsides, we drink wine and discuss regional literature, gardening, local gossip, and the Greater Good, while half-tame spotted skunks skulk in the dancing margin of firelight, hoping for a hit on the cat's food. The Gatchells moved in with Jerry's parents in 1971 to build a life in this green, placid eddy that is the Upper Smith River Valley, outside the erosional mainstream of modern life. Theater people by training, they chose temporary jobs growing fir trees in order to have time to become where they live. They know when and where most things bloom, breed, sprout, and spawn in the surrounding forest and streams. Every spring they stop using their inside fireplace so that Vaux's swifts can nest in their chimney. An aged cat sleeps in the oven of the wood-fired range. Martha and Jerry have only one obvious material weakness—books. They buy and read books voraciously, and their prodigious personal library shelves were instrumental in causing the east end of the house to sink 10 inches. Overnight.

Jerry and Martha have a passion for the past; they love this place and its history, old tools, old ways, and old trees. So Jerry is a perfect companion this morning, because the ancient Gunter orchard will die soon, and I am on a mission to save it.

This undertaking sounds dramatic, but *soon* is relative. The orchard was planted in the flat, fertile loam between Haney and Panther Creeks by my great-grandfather James Gunter, who bought a parcel of Oregon/California Railroad land in 1888, raised a house, started a family, and opened a post office and small store. As a result, you can still find "Gunter" on an Oregon highway map, but you'd better not need gas when you get there. All that remains are the old fruit trees.

James's daughter Ina was my grandmother, the second generation of Gunter inhabitants. When her second husband Grandpa Roy died in 1962, Grammy's time on "The River" ended and she moved to Eugene. No one has lived at Gunter since, and the unkempt trees are disease-ridden and toppling, usually falling in winter when rain-soaked soil can no longer hold the roots that support their unpruned, unbalanced bulk. But the death sentence for this orchard came ten years ago, a verdict handed down by the lumber company that now owns the land. They planted the flat with fast growing fir. Although the old fruit trees were left standing, they will be shaded out by the fir in the next decade or two. While I doubt that "Death by Shade" will ever become a serious drama, this is a rapid process from the perspective of a century-old orchard.

There is only one way to save an orchard, and that is to clone it. I mean this literally. Apple trees cannot be grown from seed because, like most plants and animals, every gene has two copies, one contributed by each parent. In apple trees, these two copies often differ markedly from one another. So when apple trees have sex, wild and crazy things can happen. In their seedling offspring, each of the two gene copies may end up paired with a companion gene that is different from the one that it was dancing with in the parent. This genetic do-see-doe means that seedling apple trees never end up with the same qualities as the parent tree. If that blushing, juicy, early-ripening Gravenstein beloved by everyone is allowed to plumb the depths of promiscuity, it could produce a tree with fruit resembling green, flavorless baseballs that even the bears won't touch. The only way to make a new Gravenstein is to remove a piece of one-year-old wood, a scion, from the parent and with a surgeon's care attach it to the stem of a new rootstock. With skill and luck, the cells on either side of the junction between scion and rootstock will wake up one morning, find themselves living in the same neighborhood, meet for coffee, and beneath the compelling spring sunshine decide to join forces in the common cause of healing and new growth.

Our task this morning is to search the Gunter orchard for scions. We pull into a wide spot on Smith River Road filled in along one side by buff sandstone boulders on which NO CAMPING is spray painted in white letters. Just ahead is the bridge across Haney Creek, and around the corner lies a tiny cemetery holding two earlier generations of Gunters. I slide an extension ladder out of the back of the pickup while Jerry loads a bucket with orchard tags, hammer, nails, and plastic bags for scions. We step off the road onto a game trail leading through an otherwise impenetrable wall of blackberries, Scotch broom, and young fir trees. Several seedling apples have sprung up next to the road, probably descendents of the original orchard that have sprouted from seeds excreted by an overfull bear on his way up Haney Creek at the end of an autumn night. One of these seedlings produces beautiful fruit that hangs from the tree like gaudy pink tear drops. They taste terrible.

The trail tunnels into the brushy dimness. Elk droppings, shiny and olive green, are strewn along the way, and the faint scent of large ungulates clings to the undergrowth around us; they were here last night. We step over a pile of decomposing bear manure full of last fall's apples. The ladder is cumbersome, almost too long for the narrow, winding corridor. Wet dead fir needles dislodge from branches next to the trail, sticking to the back of my neck like skinny brown insects.

Shortly, the overgrown path emerges into an opening guarded by a gangly three-story pear tree. The fallen pears are huge and green, and only now, in February, have they begun to rot. This is a "pound," a centuries-old culinary pear variety. Grammy used to complain bitterly about a "pear that never got ripe." Apparently her father hadn't told her that the fibrous fruit was meant only for baking. This one small forgotten thing is cause for humility, especially in the heady days of the Information Age where we pride ourselves on our rapidly accumulating knowledge. Perhaps we might pause and consider the knowledge that we have lost.

Our path veers right and delivers us beneath two of the original apple trees. They are a Gravenstein and a Rhode Island Greening, the only varieties in this orchard that I have identified. Both trees are huge, and the Gravenstein is exceptionally tall. Yet they are no longer grand. Their limbs are leafless and covered with long gray Beard Lichen. Many branches are broken. The trees remind me of two old men standing on the same front porch day after day, friends who will never be parted, too tired to care any longer about appearances. I post the ladder against the massive trunk of the Greening, and the shiny aluminum seems too bright against the dark bark. The trunk is riddled with tiny holes from a Red-breasted Sapsucker, a small scarlet-headed wood-pecker that drills into the sap-bearing wood to drink the sugary liquid and capture bugs stuck in the ooze. The broken branches indicate that bears have enjoyed this tree for years, including last fall. I once read that a bear will happily prune a fruit tree for you; that humans keep the bears out, then have to prune the trees themselves, an example of how deluded humans are. But they're *bears* fergodsake, with an even shorter, more self-centered, and brutish vision for the future than most of us. They climb to the safety of a large, unbreakable limb, and eat by reaching outward to pull the fruit-bearing branches toward them, often breaking the tree in haphazard ways. I prefer to do my own pruning.

Still, the bear's destructive shortsightedness has helped me this morning. The unkempt Greening has mustered enough gumption to respond to the insult of broken limbs by sending out a dozen new suckers about two feet long spanning a range of diameters roughly the same as my fingers. The shoots are covered with thin green bark as tender as baby skin. They are perfect. I pull out my orange-handled loppers and snip off six sci-ons, letting them slip from my hand and fall into the wet, brown grass. Jerry inscribes the numeral "1" into the soft metal of an orchard tag and anchors it to the trunk with a nail. I find my way out of the tree without breaking my own limbs, while he retrieves the scions and wraps the cut ends in a plastic bag also labeled "1". This Rhode Island Greening, ancient, gnarly, and broken, supporter of generations of sapsuckers and bears and Gunters, has been efficiently reduced to a handful of pencil-thin wood called Tree #1. We'll return in the fall to pick the apples and have their identity confirmed by an apple expert. This will be a grafting of old knowledge onto new rootstock.

Jerry and I fall into something of a sylvicultural rhythm as we move from tree to tree; I climb and cut, he collects and labels. Some trees are besieged by thorny blackberries, and I use loppers and leather gloves to cut the brambles and pull them out of the way. Tree #8 has fallen but is not dead, and its scions can be cut without climbing. A patch of new stinging nettle shoots, deep green and two inches high, have sprouted under tree #10. We stop to pick some for dinner, sacrificing a plastic scion bag to carry them. Tree #12 is so near death that the only new growth hangs precariously at the end of a branch two stories off the ground. I can only reach these scions by fully extending the ladder and placing it directly against the limb, which sways perilously as I climb. But apple wood is tough stuff and it bears my weight. Jerry logs the position of each tree into his GPS. He is a walking mix of modern and ancient technology, proof that we can love old orchards and grafting and still use computers and aluminum ladders, all with the same brain.

Navy blue Steller's Jays call from a ridge above us. With alternating swoops and glides they descend to the knoll, where the two-story gray house once stood, to search for any remaining nuts in the remnants of the filbert orchard. I dimly remember filberts drying in trays around the woodstove, a burlap bag half-full of nuts leaning against the wall. For decades the filbert trees have cloned themselves, sending suckers up from their spreading roots, and these have in turn grown their own roots, so that now each original tree has become an outwardly expanding cluster of trees. Last winter Kim and I visited the knoll, removed some of the newly rooted suckers, and transplanted them to the last family-owned place on Smith River, the Johnny Gunter property twelve miles upstream. Peer closely into the center of each filbert clump, and the broken, decaying stub of the parent can still be seen watching from within.

Morning transitions seamlessly, timelessly into afternoon. The temperature is unchanged. A single vehicle has passed during the entire day; there is little reason to be this far from home on a weekend in February. Jerry and I have collected scions from fourteen trees, and fatigue is sneaking up on me like a stalking cat. I slip into introspection that becomes an odd mix of satisfaction and self-doubt. Why am I doing this? Why am I spending my birthday climbing and crawling and cutting, slipping in composting bear scat, swinging from wet branches two stories up? Yes, some very old heirloom apple varieties might be saved, a small statement in opposition to a huge system of industrial fruit production that prizes the qualities of storage, shipping, and uniformity over flavor and genetic diversity. I could have asked for a birthday present of scions from an heirloom orchard company. But they wouldn't have been these scions, from this orchard, from these trees, that were planted by my great-grandfather's hands.

Of course my grafting project won't save this orchard, any more than swirling some of my cells in a tube and growing someone genetically identical to me would make a new me. I can't replicate James Gunter's hope and vision for the future as he walked into the winter rain falling on newly cleared ground, dug each hole, inserted the young trees, carefully spread their new roots, then covered them with sandy soil. He loved trees, and the particular satisfaction that he must have felt as each sapling leafed out in the sunshine of the following spring is gone now. He would have strode out during ensuing winters, pruning saw and loppers in hand, making just the right cuts to shape each growing tree. Only in this orchard would he have picked boxes of fall apples, wondering if sons Francis, Victor, and Paul would survive the bloody trenches of World War I. Only this orchard has seen black bears steal out of Haney Creek canyon in the cool autumn darkness, clamber upward, and crunch ripe apples, cider dribbling out the corners of their long mouths.

Only this orchard has seen these things in this place in this time. The orchard is an individual thing, and like all individuals—a rock, plant, or human—it had a beginning and it will have an end. I will grow a new orchard from these trees, a seed will germinate, a baby will be born, and sand will be pressed into a new rock. But none of these things will be equivalent to their predecessors. So why persist in "saving" an orchard that cannot be truly saved? Because this orchard has roots in the soil that connect me to my roots. Ten years of academic transiency honed my intellectual skills but did nothing to plant and nurture me, nothing to anchor me. Now I can climb lichen-covered apple trees, look west across Haney Creek to where my ancestors are buried, to the place where they were returned to this ground. Regrowing these old trees is a continuation of memory, an extension of this place, my place.

But here's the rub. These things that produce the fruit of memory cannot last. All of them are individuals that will die, and their energy will become something else. How can we let them go so that they can assume their larger role in the universe and yet hold them in our memories so that they illuminate our past, fix us in the present, and allow us to step into an otherwise uncertain future? I'm not sure. But intuitively I suspect that resolving this conundrum has to do with joy, and whether our memories make us glad to be here. Right now. Today I can hope that a new orchard will grow, long beyond the time that I no longer exist as this particular version of matter. I can believe that my descendents will pick fruit from the new old trees, knowing that these apples came from ancients now gone. I can trust that the people who come after me will remember that funny old guy who grew the trees and thought that in some way old orchards never die.

Two weeks before the summer solstice, cold rain falls like an unshakable bad habit, gray runoff sluicing down the gutter along our suburban street. Three months have passed since I grafted the Gunter orchard onto rootstocks purchased at the local Seed and Scion Swap. The best scions were cut and carefully size-matched to each stem rising from the new root wad. The junctions were wrapped with electrician's tape, and these wannabe trees were planted in black gallon-size pots. They now line the edge of the driveway, silhouetted against our cedar fence like the stick figures that children draw. I shrug off the unseasonably icy raindrops and visit each of my infant trees as though wandering through an open-air maternity ward. On twelve grafts, pale green leaves, each tender as a newborn's ear, have erupted from the old wood.

FILTHY STINKING RICH

In western Oregon our passage from winter to spring is a long slow hike marked only by the rain gradually becoming a few degrees warmer. My friend Ken and I know this in our bones. We shrug and slide from the dull warmth of the pickup into the windy bite of a morning squall and stand at the roadside pullout looking down on Coos Bay spreading east and west below us. Low tide on an estuarine mudflat is a foraging shorebird probing every crevice of the senses. Cold, wet bugs of spring rain pelt our faces while screeching gulls ply the wind through a sky of molten lead on platinum. Our eyes reach wide to pull in the vast expanse of bay bottom: ashen silt still wet from the receding tide, small whitecaps on steely water, and great egrets stalking daintily across the muck as though one false step would utterly ruin their white feathers.

But the overriding sensation is the reek of rotten eggs. The moon has drawn the bay water back into the Pacific Ocean, exposing an immense quantity of pungent mud that unleashes hydrogen sulfide, a gas by-product of microbes busily dismantling once-living tissue that has settled to the bottom of the estuary, reducing what was alive to its elemental form, preparing it to become something new. It is the stench of death, but only in an immediate sense. Ultimately, it's the aroma of an ecosystem throbbing with life.

We stand for a moment, swirling the scene in a crystal glass, holding it to the light, watching its essence crawl down clear sides. At first we carefully taste. Then we dive in, hopelessly drunk. Pulling on waders and rain jackets, we drag out five-gallon buckets, metal handles snapping on hard plastic, grab our shovels, and bail off the road, negotiating a steep path lined with bent spruce and salal. The trail deposits us onto the tidal flat, and we continue onward toward the quietly receding edge of water a quarter-mile distant. On dry ground this would be an easy stroll, but the muck slurps at our boots, making our trek a laborious slog.

Ken grew up in a foraging family and would probably weigh only one hundred pounds had wild food been removed from his household. Shorter and stockier than I, his forearms are still strong from throwing hay bales for summer money when he was a teenager. We met in junior high band class, and he is the only person from my school days with whom I've managed to stay in contact. When Kim and I were living in St. Louis raising two young children and chasing a career 2,000 miles from a tidal estuary, we vacationed in Oregon. On that trip Ken didn't tell me to move home; he just took me fishing in our old places and reminded me how rich life could be here. We returned to Oregon a year later. Since then I've gone clam digging with others, but usually they only come once. Ken is the only person who continues to accompany me.

Swapping dimensions, I trudge back in time, dredging the accumulated sediment of memory to retrieve my first clam tide. It was a spring weekend, and the adults of my extended family were digging deeply, trying to re-connect with what they had known. Ten years earlier my maternal step-grandfather Grandpa Roy had suddenly left us. Roy had come to love seafood in his days as a mail carrier along Oregon's south coast. He knew the best places: not restaurants, but spots where shellfish could be foraged in abundance. His death rent a gaping hole in the family that no amount of wishing could mend, and now the next generation was working to re-member what he had shared.

On that weekend in my youth, the adults found the pullout at the end of the short road, helped the kids make the hike along the railroad bed and negotiate the scary trestle across a muddy channel, and broke trail through tall rushes to the mud where the softshell clams lived. We kids were happy as pigs in a wallow, reveling in those rare few hours when we were allowed to get com-pletely filthy. At the end of the weekend we stopped at Uncle Dick's to shuck the clams, and the adults huddled once more, collectively remembering how Roy had made his clam fritters. Mom later enshrined the recipe in the Family Cookbook. Years afterward I returned from the Midwest with my own family, and Alex and Laurel began making the hike across the trestle, learning to excavate softshells from the muck. Thus, memory continues.

This morning Ken and I scan the sooty silt before us, pockmarked with holes in the way that old apple trees are riddled with sapsucker drills. Each dimpled opening in the mud is an airway to something living, some subterranean secret: a sand shrimp, a marine worm, or a clam, all of them biding their time, waiting for the return of the water. For clams, the holes are where the "neck" extends above the mud when the tide is in. This neck is actually a siphon used to suck in water laden with food particles. The clams filter out the nutrients within their soft bodies then expel the filtered water back into the bay. The mudflat is populated by sensuous butter clams with pink crenulated lips bulging from between their shells, light-colored cockles incised with ridges as deep and steep as the coastal mountains, and littleneck clams the color of weathered basalt, with finer ridges that make them look like prepubescent cockles. They have partitioned the space among them as roommates would share a house, each species living at a different depth in the mud or distance from shore.

All of these are great food when steamed, fried, chopped, and chowdered. But gapers are the real trophies on this mudflat. They "gape" because their necks are so long and large that the two halves of their shell must form an opening around the thick base. Gaper holes are easy to find. They are oblong and large, sometimes an inch in diameter, and when you stick your finger into one, the leathery end of the siphon can be felt retreating, sometimes sending a stream of water upward like a disturbed subterranean penis. These clams aren't just endowed with a spectacularly large siphon; the rest of the clam is big as well, weighing up to a couple of pounds, and from a forager's perspective this is a lot of potential clam fritter. The downside is that gapers *are* down, sometimes two feet down in that malodorous mud, which translates into a lot of hard, dirty work on the end of a shovel, a form of recreational stoop labor. The legal limit is only twelve gapers per person, a number that is certainly consistent with the limitations imposed upon Ken and me by our aging backs.

We are not alone on the mudflat. At least a dozen other people have come to dig on the morning minus tide, so we politely adjust our route to separate ourselves from the couple closest to us, find a cluster of siphon holes, and begin digging. Ken's shovel bites decisively into the mud, and he scoops out heaps of watery muck using only his arm strength. Pushing aside a clump of eel grass lying on the mud, I find an especially large hole and begin digging.

Excavating a gaper isn't mindless. Water immediately begins to seep into the depression, forming a slurry at the bottom. After removing a few shovelfuls of silt, I stick a finger into the hole, feeling for the retracted neck, possibly even the top of the shell. In spite of their large size, gaper shells are fragile and break like china when struck with a shovel blade. The slatey grit stains my hands, forcing its way under my fingernails and cuticles. My left index finger finds a fragment of old shell somewhere in the bottom of the deepening pit. I don't immediately feel the burn of the cut because my hands are cold, but dark blood begins oozing out, mixing with the grime, dripping into the hole. My arms are soon soaked to the pits. There is no particular hurry when digging a gaper, other than the impending tide. Unlike razor clams that actively dig downward into the sand, gapers stay put, counting instead on being buried so deeply that would-be clam predators simply give up. We often do give up, sometimes losing track of the siphon hole in the watery sludge. Yet this time the clam is worth the energy. Digging past one side of the shell, I work my bloody fingers around both sides, gently rocking, carefully loosening its grip on the bay bottom to avoid breaking it. The gaper finally pops free. I swish off the excess mud in the water that has collected at the bottom of the pit. For a moment I admire my prize, the gray and white shell with concentric oval ridges, the thick neck covered with brown boot-leather skin, the heft in my hand. The clam makes a satisfying clunk in my empty bucket. Eleven more to go before water reclaims the flat.

At times I've wondered whether the cumulative effect of our yearly clam harvest is a long-term danger to gaper populations. Clams don't strike me as able to do anything very quickly. Does it take fifty years to grow an adult gaper? Will they become the passenger pigeon of the Pacific, the bison of Coos Bay? Will we dig them into oblivion, twelve clams at a time? One day I phoned the Oregon Department of Fish and Wildlife shellfish biologist, my integrity on the line. He told me that gapers are full-grown after only six years and many clams are never uncovered even at the lowest tides, so there is a continuous source of clams from which to resupply the entire bay. Gapers are very good at making more gapers; in late winter females produce thousands of eggs and males churn out millions of sperm, releasing them through the outgoing plumbing of their siphons directly into the water. The shellfish biologist seemed to feel a little guilty that gaper numbers were so easy to manage. I felt absolved.

The mudflat begins to look like a bombing range, with pits and piles of muck scattered haphazardly across the glistening surface. Gulls move in to scavenge the piles. Our buckets become heavy with large clams. My arms are heavy, too, and carry on them the living odor of the estuary. The squall has blown eastward, transporting its rain to the coastal mountains, and the tide begins its slow return, filling the low places around us with lapping water. Ken and I joke about a short story we read in junior high school English class, "The Ledge" by Lawrence Sargent Hall, in which a man and two boys are stranded on a coastal island while duck hunting and eventually drown in the high tide. This isn't a funny tale, and our chuckle is a combination of dark humor and some tension from the accumulated close calls of our youth. A little fear is the mother of common sense.

We stop next to a shallow channel now growing relentlessly as the hands of the moon smooth the bulge of offshore water, spreading the gray quilt of ocean back across the bay bottom. Emptying the clams from our buckets, we rinse and count them. I check my cut index finger; the creases on my left palm are thin ash-colored rivers running westward with heart and life lines forming a confluence at the coastline just above my thumb. The bleeding stopped two hours earlier.

I try to stretch my tired arms around this estuary, attempt to appreciate all that it offers. Some years ago I encountered a modern, anthropocentric concept of abundance, ironically when our family finances were at low ebb. In those days I learned that the dominant culture tends to view abundance along only a single axis: the accumulation of stuff, especially expensive stuff. The Masters, our moral teachers, have always known that material and spiritual abundance can be at odds. Yet I wonder if we have oversimplified our view of materialism by losing sight of the connection between the things with which we surround ourselves and our biological support system. This artificial separation, created only in our minds, defies any true understanding of the *ecological* abundance that makes any level of material existence possible.

Ecologies are complex webs of interaction between all kinds of things, both living and nonliving. They are bays full of microbes and plants and animals that harvest sunlight or eat other things and then die and smell like rotten eggs and become yet other things that are evolving under the influence of tides generated by moon and sun, earth and water. In my outstretched mind I try to comprehend the reality that my physical being is derived from this estuary, from this earth, rather than the local big box store. This is a truth that is easily forgotten.

The Coos, Coquille, Lower Umpqua, and Siuslaw peoples did not forget. Their shellfish middens are deep and their memories deeper still of abundant clam tides over the millennia. This direct connection with the source of their food over thousands of generations has given them an appreciation of their dependence on the estuary and the place of humans on earth. This attitude has produced a culture of gratitude for seasonal reliability, a bay teeming with high quality protein on those special tides that come when days lengthen, maples and alders burst with new leaves, and wild rhododendrons are adorned with voluptuous pink flowers.

My cultural connection to clam digging is only four generations deep, shallow in comparison, and was nearly uprooted half a century ago when Roy unexpectedly died. But his spirit remained as a seed that the next generation planted and nurtured, and it grew into something important and enduring. For a time this living part of me became landlocked and dormant. Then it leafed out and bloomed again under the tug of an old friend, family, and the invisible force of the spring moon.

Ken and I return the rinsed clams to our buckets and slog toward shore, the pickup, home, and Grandpa

Roy's clam fritters. Turning inward, I wonder if I live my life in a manner worthy of the cyclical dependability of this estuary, of the biosphere. The answer is less important than the asking, because the question moves me beyond the prevalent idea that I am in some way destined to exploit this planet. Humans *are* different from eel grass, clams, and gulls. This is biological reality. But our differences do not confer upon us some special status, a license to take without giving. Perhaps the time has come for an opening of clenched hands, releasing the notion that somehow we deserve our lives, surrounded and supported by other life, on this blue rock hurtling through space.

BEEING HERE

All I wanted was a fifty-pound bag of oats.

Winter was over and my stash of rolled oats was gone, transformed into oatmeal, apple crisp, and peanut butter–chocolate chip cookies. When my rolled oats are gone, I become as edgy as a gray squirrel without acorns. But I am not an elegant forager; I don't leap gracefully through white oak and fir, belly flashing like white lightning just ahead of a spectacular silver tail. Rather, I get into my ordinary pickup, drive across a drab, light-industrial area of west Eugene to GloryBee Foods, a local bulk food supplier, and plop down some money.

Arriving on their doorstep on a sunny Saturday morning in mid-April, I was greeted by a locked entrance. Karen, a pleasant middle-aged woman, materialized from the depths of their small retail shop, pushed open the door, and stood amid an aromatic cloud of spices and candle scents.

"Are you here for bees?" she asked.

"Uh, no. Just a bag of rolled oats."

"Well, our retail store isn't open on weekends," she cheerfully replied. "We're only in today because people are picking up their bees."

Not open on Saturday? My thoughts adjusted slowly to this news. Even in laid-back Eugene, Oregon, the gods of capitalism dictate that any store intent on surviving in the world of "free" enterprise damn well better be open on weekends. Most folks are too busy the rest of the week making money to actually spend it. Nevertheless, Karen clearly had no intention of selling me rolled oats this morning.

"Do you have a copy of our catalog?" she asked.

Silently I wondered if the catalog had a price for Saturday rolled oats. "I don't believe I do," was my reply.

"If you'd like to wait a minute, I'll go inside and see if I can find one for you."

My irritation subsided, giving way to a sort of mental flux that occurs when my brain cells gather themselves before flying off in a new direction. Mental billiards: action and reaction, but without the predictability.

"Sure, that'd be great," I mumbled absentmindedly.

Karen disappeared behind a glass door, which reflected the image of a small parking lot immediately behind me. The catalogs must have been misplaced, because she seemed to be taking an eternity. She was probably gone for only three minutes, but this was one of those moments when the arbitrariness of time disappears and the future hangs in breathless balance. A lot of thoughts can roll and ricochet off the bumpers of my brain in the space of three minutes; dangerous, life-changing thoughts. I was no longer thinking about rolled oats.

She returned with my catalog.

"So you sell beekeeping stuff?" I inquired.

I suppose my question should have elicited something sarcastic like "Let's see, our company name *is* GloryBee, which might imply that we do indeed have some interest in bees and the like ..."

But Karen was polite. "We do. This weekend people are picking up their orders of honeybees to start their hives. That's the only reason we're open today."

"Really?"

Dad and I had been kicking the beekeeping idea around for several years now. Mom had inherited five acres from her Uncle Johnny in the Upper Smith River Valley of the Oregon Coast Range. He had kept bees for much of his four decades there, and before falling ill and moving to a care facility in town, he had given Mom some raw honeycomb that Kim and I tasted while we were visiting from Kansas. The honey was thick, dark, and richly aromatic, as though it had seeped from the soul of the forest surrounding Johnny's hives. Standing in the GloryBee parking lot years later, that taste became a cue stick that sent my neurons clicking and bouncing on some collective trajectory that constitutes memory. Now that we were back in Oregon for the long haul, I was looking for excuses to indulge my penchant for growing food, tending to my literal and metaphorical roots.

Karen continued. "Well, if you're interested, now would be a good time. We have five demonstration hives that were set up to teach people how to install their bees, and they're a hundred and ten dollars. It's a good deal and a good way to get started."

Following was a rare moment when I fought down reckless impulse. The only reason I didn't say yes immediately was because I needed Mom and Dad's okay.

"Can I get back to you Monday morning?" I asked.

Mom and Dad were happy to have bees on the Smith River place again, so when Monday morning arrived I was back at GloryBee to pay for the hive. It was mine only on paper, though. I was unschooled in the ways of bees, and a lot can go wrong with a new hive. It needed to be tended for a month by someone who knew what they are doing so the new colony could establish a field force large enough for the hive to become self-sufficient.

I did have visitation rights, though, and Karen led me to the back of a large freight lot. On the black asphalt was a white pine box about the size of an orange crate. My bees were traveling in and out through a narrow slit in the bottom of the front panel. We chatted for a few minutes about how wonderful bees are. They are the archetype of cooperation and connectedness. Tens of thousands of individuals perform very specialized tasks within the hive, so tightly knit by complex behavioral and chemical communication that they seem to perform as a single organism. In our culture we are taught to admire them for their industry, their tireless "busy-as-a-bee" devotion to duty. We allude to people we love as "honey." Yet we seem to be of two minds about bees and often denigrate their cooperation. "Hive mentality" represents an unquestioning, unflinching devotion to one's role in society, especially work, that places us at risk of becoming socially engineered tools of someone's larger plan. Bees are protective of their hive, and god knows they sting; hence we refer to someone as "angry as a swarm of bees." But the bees couldn't care less about our anthropomorphic take on their existence. They simply do what has worked for them for 40 million years.

"We'll give you a call when they're ready," Karen said.

I had a lot to learn and began by reading a copy of *First Lessons in Beekeeping* by C. P. Dadant (original copyright 1917) that Dad had retrieved from Uncle Johnny's belongings. The pages were coming loose and were as stiff and yellow around the edges as an old cigarette smoker's fingers. The photographs were black and white and grainy and had no women in them. Cosmetics aside, the book was as timeless as the 40-million-year biology of honeybees, and I was heartened by the title of Chapter 1: "Beekeeping Is Pleasurable and Profitable."

Girded with new knowledge, I met Karen in the parking lot on a sunny mid-May morning. A strip of wood had been nailed over the hive entrance at dawn, trapping the inhabitants for the one-hour ride to the Johnny Gunter place. Karen used a cart to wheel the hive over to my pickup and we slid it into the back, safely enclosed within the canopy top. After the bees were loaded, the financial reality of keeping them alive began to sink in. I still needed a head net, protective gloves, smoker, hive tool, bee brush, and at least one more pine box with honey frames to expand the hive as it grew. This set me back another two hundred bucks, almost twice the cost of the bees themselves. I winced, wrote the check, and hit the road. Money and I have parted company more often than not, and we rarely seem to miss one another. Pleasurable and profitable.

This morning was at least pleasurable, one of those irreplaceable spring days that cause western Oregonians to strain at the leash. In May the rains finally taper off, and sunshine reveals an insurgence of green that seems to have developed underground, waiting for this moment to leap from beneath the wet blanket of March and April to take winter out by force. Roadside grasses suddenly become tall and top-heavy under the weight of their oblong, green flower heads, ready to send clouds of pollen into the warm air and the waiting lungs of the allergy-afflicted. Along waterways the gallery forests of big-leaf maple, cottonwood, and alder leaf out, enveloping purple larkspur, pink bleeding hearts, and white cow parsnip in a shady embrace. This botanical madness infests every living thing in the countryside, and I succumb more easily than most to the temporary insanity. My place comes with rain-filled winters that I have come to embrace as a time for rest and introspection. But when sunny spring days increase in frequency, the pace of my life quickens, driven especially by the demands of gardening. Some folks call this manic. I call it staying in tune.

There are two ways to the Johnny Gunter place. One is a slow ramble on winding two-lane country roads, shorter by distance but more time-consuming. The other is a faster but longer freeway route with little to offer other than speed. This morning my cargo demanded expediency, and I turned onto Interstate 5 and drove south.

About twenty minutes later, somewhere between Cottage Grove and Curtin, I looked in the rear view mirror and saw perhaps twenty escaped bees circling within the enclosed canopy. The miles were flying by and the bees were flying as well, the number of escapes steadily increasing. This shouldn't have been happening. When I left Karen in Eugene there had been a strip of wood *nailed* across the hive opening. Bees don't pull nails. Then I realized that my newly purchased protective gear was also in the back. With the escaped bees.

I took a deep, diaphragmatic breath and kept driving. Exiting the southern end of the Willamette Valley, we began the descent down Pass Creek, once an important Native American route into the Umpqua River drainage. This stretch of the freeway follows a corridor of red alders with silver gray trunks that grow straight and smooth to high branches with dark green leaves. The alders lean slightly inward, as though biding their time, knowing that someday they will reclaim this four-lane scar of concrete and pavement. Turning west along Highway 38, I wondered what the driver of the large semi-truck behind me would think if he knew that the pickup in front of him had been taken over by honeybees and was becoming a sixty-mile-per-hour hive.

Upper Smith River Road twists into the Coast Range like honey drizzling onto warm bread. Creeping around the second climbing hairpin turn at fifteen miles per hour we passed an old Douglas fir tree conspicuously tall amid the young second growth and roadside brush. A crack had formed about ten feet up the trunk, a scar that opened into the heart of the tree. Feral honeybees had recently moved in, and at my slow speed they could be seen from the road, entering and exiting the crack like miniature bats swirling around the mouth of a cave.

Without help these feral bees would be unlikely to survive. In 1987, seventy years after Dadant penned *First Lessons*, a tiny parasitic mite appropriately named *Varroa destructor* arrived in North America from east Asia. It spread rapidly and began literally sucking the life out of hives across the continent. The mite is a miniscule bee vampire, attaching itself to the body and removing the hemolymph, which is analogous to our blood. This blood-sucking behavior eventually weakens the bee such that it can no longer forage. Too many mites on too many workers eventually results in too little nectar returning to the hive and starvation for the entire colony. A few bee strains are mite resistant, but the majority require human help to control their tormentors. Twenty years after the initial mite invasion, a handful of wild hives are now beginning to persist, suggesting that bees with innate mite resistance are becoming part of the undomesticated landscape. The Big Tree Hive might make it, but the odds are poor.

The wild hive disappeared as I rounded the next bend. My truck full of discombobulated bees snaked across the ridge tops then descended into the headwaters of Smith River. The single lane driveway to the Johnny Gunter place turns upward to the right, angling into a shady tunnel of second growth fir, two ruts separated by grass and wild iris. Unlocking the rusty gate, I pulled into the sun drenched meadow, still green from spring rains.

Johnny Gunter spent his life on Smith River. He was married for a short time but ended up a bachelor for most of his years. In 1948 his older brother Marion deeded five acres to him, and Johnny built a small house with the help of my paternal grandfather Roland Titus, planted apples trees, and set himself there for the rest of his days. The fruit trees were now in full bloom on both sides of the driveway. To the right, two long outbuildings perch just outside the upper orchard fence, with traces of weathered red paint on rough gray siding that leans toward the fruit trees. Between the sheds is a cinderblock root cellar dug into the bank, the roof partly covered with vines of wild sweet pea sporting pink leguminous flowers.

To the left of the driveway stands the old house. A new green metal roof rests incongruously on walls sided with old cedar shakes that at one time were red but have gradually been transformed into a subdued salmon color under several decades of incessant winter rain. A few shingles have fallen. Many have small holes that are home to a healthy population of native mason bees, who were about to be imposed upon by my nonindigenous European honeybees, yet another hybrid ecology produced by agricultural humans. You just can't get honey from mason bees.

On the side of the house facing the driveway is a double hung window, the lower half broken and boarded over. Inside the glass of the intact upper half is an old cardboard sign with hand-drawn black letters, now faded and nearly invisible:

> NO TRESPASSING
> I NEVER COME HERE UNARMED
> IT WILL BE A SAD DAY FOR ANY
> SONOFABITCH I CATCH HERE

Beyond the house, the driveway expands into a parking area, and behind this the meadow slopes gradually upward. I made a climbing, sweeping rightward arc that deposited the truck at the gate to the upper orchard. Fetching a shovel from inside the house, I dug out a level place under an apple tree in the center of the orchard. According to my books this would be a good spot for the hive. With the entrance facing east the bees would be

warmed by the morning sun and protected from storms
coming from the southwest. The apple tree would provide some overhead shade during the heat of summer,
and a deer fence encircling the orchard would at least
discourage bears. On the leveled ground I turned four
cinder blocks on end, the foundation for the hive. The
cinder blocks would raise the box high enough so that
skunks, which scratch at the hive entrance at night to
roust out bees and eat them, would have to stand on
their hind legs and expose their underbellies to bee
stings.

The bees were waiting. Although a little procrastina-
tion is sometimes a healthy coping strategy, no more di-
versionary chores came to mind. At least one hundred
disconcerted apian souls were circling inside the pickup
canopy and clinging pathetically to the window screens.
Looking through the canopy window I saw that the bee
box had slid somewhat toward the front, then realized
that the lid had shifted slightly ajar in transit, explaining
the escapees. "*If you keep bees you will be stung,*" warned the
books. Steeling myself, I quickly flipped open the canopy door and retrieved gloves, hat, and head net, then
slammed the door, all without incident. My protective
gear was embarrassingly pristine and newbie white. But
no one was there to laugh, and I gratefully pulled on all
of the clothing. Fully girded, I slid out the hive box with
who knew how many bees still inside and immediately
reset the lid. The box was heavy and I hugged it against
my body with both arms in the way that I once carried
my newborn children from the hospital. Toting the box
to the apple tree, I set it gently on the cinder blocks and
then raised the back corners a little with bits of old cedar
shingle so that the rain would run off the front.

At this juncture, naïve would be a polite description of my position on the beekeeping learning curve, a gross understatement of my emerging ignorance. One hundred bees inside my pickup canopy seemed like a lot, so I decided to satisfy my curiosity and see how many were actually left inside the bee box. Carefully lifting the lid about six inches, I gazed in on what might have been a scene from the *X-Files*. Most of what were likely 10,000 bees remained home, and the writhing mass of insects was more than my untrained brain could effectively process. I dropped the lid shut as though the box contained poisonous gas. In the world of bees, one hundred isn't really very many.

The time had come for the official release. With my virgin hive tool I pried off the wood strip over the entrance and retreated a few steps. Bees immediately moved onto the two-inch landing porch, walking in circles. Then they began to launch in twos and threes, spiraling upward on their navigational flight, ascending through pink and white apple blossoms into blue skies, queuing off the warm May sunshine, searching for nectar.

We were all getting our bearings.

PRELUDE TO LOGGING

Anger would have been easier.

But they were so nice, so neighborly. They smiled and joked and told us how quickly it would be done, how light would inundate the meadow, how deer and elk would come, how fast trees grow. They told us that it's always been this way. Afterward, I mow three nonstop acres of knapweed, bracken, grass, and gopher mounds, my grief exploding in two-foot swaths under the spinning blades, mow around a man-forest of well-spaced apple trees, mow until the sun drops behind the western tree line soon to be stump line, mow until the engine starves and my exhausted hands have choked it all into submission and release the dead handle and sweat-tears beneath my temples cool into streaks of gritty sorrow.

But I am not angry.

Darkness wraps newborn spring in its soft blanket. Light seeping in around loose untucked edges illuminates an earthbound galaxy of four-petaled dogwood stars shining over the collapsed cabin where forty years past Uncle Francis slept forever. They found this funny, too.

Great Horned Owl shouts from a jagged shadow of conifers on the ridge behind, trees I could have been buried under. From the darkening canyons of my mind I see the owl's pale throat puffing out in utter defiance, dotted eighth-sixteenth-quarter-quarter-quarter. Hoos in four, andante. Or is it a question? Whose? Whose trees casting shades of green wandering from yellow to black and back again? Whose deer mice with small night eyes, rustling in the duff, visible only to owl's ears? Whose cool tongues of dew-laden air reaching outward from forest to meadow, licking my salty neck with evening, brushing wild iris petals with lavender inscribed in white feathers? Whose deepening memories you found so amusing?

Pygmy Owl answers from the blackness of the creek bottom, a plaintive monotonic "toot," the sound of the high lead whistle after choker setters scramble and another round of naked trees is drug to the landing to trucks to mill to pallets neatly stacked with blond freshly cut two-by-fours, sticky with kiln-dried tree blood, smelling of sweet turpentine. Sixty for $1.89 each at the two-by-four store framed my shed, finished just before the autumn rains, now filled with a cider press and canning jars, family wages and college funds, private jets and race horses, Our Way of Life and a War on Everything.

Whose? Whose water burbling from the mountain's cracked heart into a two-gallon pool, tickling the feet of lady ferns, trickling over moss-pillowed rocks into the white porcelain cup holding a half-grown torrent salamander with olive flanks of weathered sandstone, patiently waiting? Returned to the spring, she watches me from water's edge with dark upturned eyes just breaking the crystalline surface. Is this the face of gratitude? Dipping gently, icy water spills inward leaving Salamander undisturbed as bits of rotting leaf and wood dance in the small current, swirling across brown-beige-yellow-ocher pebbles. Each cold-blooded mouthful slips off my tongue and slithers downward, coming to rest in a cool ball in my center, waiting, yearning to be born as wind on owl wings.

I am not angry.

SMITH RIVER MEMORIAL GARDEN

In the long run the land will heal and so will I. But right now there is no poetry left on the hillside above my garden. There will be no shadows growing into evening, no owls calling from dark depths of the forest, no tiny calypso orchids exuding sex from bulbous pink blossoms rising out of thick moss. This altered landscape has no depth aesthetically, ecologically, or geometrically. What remains is a two-dimensional battlefield of broken fir parts, some scattered haphazardly across injured soil, others pushed into piles awaiting cremation. Interspersed are the stumps, with growth rings that write a cross-sectional epitaph to trees now gone. When the ground dries I will drive out on the clearcut and rummage the remains for useable firewood. High above, a group of seven ravens cavort in spinning dives on the southwest wind of an incoming storm. Ravens can apparently find joy anywhere.

My garden, a 30- by 45-foot plot on the knoll just west of the Johnny Gunter cabin, is one immediate beneficiary in all of the destruction. The treeless western horizon is now significantly lower and the evening sun will rest on the meadow for longer each day, keeping the soil warm and making it a more hospitable place for the heat-loving crops that I grow here: corn, squash, beans, and tomatoes. I would gladly have traded my garden for an intact forest, but such a transaction was never to be. Owls and orchids do not figure into the cold calculus of board feet in the timber economy.

The garden was born in 1999 in anticipation of the supposed worldwide computer meltdown that would meet us at Y2K and put an immediate end to globalized food production. That spring, Dad and I found the place between Uncle Johnny's house and Uncle Francis's abandoned one-room cabin where the ground sloped very gently downhill to the east. The soil here seemed deeper and more level than in other places nearby. Although there was no trace of a fence or any cultivation, Dad remembered that this was where Johnny and Francis had shared a vegetable garden.

We drove stakes in the corners and plowed the grass and knapweed under with Dad's small garden tractor. Kim and I shaped the tilled earth into five beds, each about five feet wide, while Dad found the buried water line coming from the springhouse hidden in the old growth forest up the hill. He tapped into the pipe and placed a faucet at one corner of the rectangle. Because I didn't care to share the fruits and vegetables of my agrarian labor with the deer, I scavenged some rusty, eight-foot woven wire fencing, stretched it around the garden on red and white metal posts, and finished the enclosure with an old gate that someone had fabricated from metal pipe and more woven wire. In the fall we harvested a large crop of corn, squash, and potatoes. But at 12:01 a.m., January 1, 2000, the computers kept computing, the lights kept lighting, and the frenzy that we euphemistically call "modern life" continued to careen wildly into a fully automated if altogether uncertain future.

Blessed with any common sense whatsoever, I would have rolled up the deer fence and abandoned the garden on January 2. But who aspires to being common? To my knowledge I own the county record for "distance traveled to place of food production." From my house in Eugene, the garden is 35 miles by the short, time-consuming, pretty way and 45 miles by the long, fast, freeway route. Confessing this to my food-growing acquaintances, especially the hard core advocates for sustainability, sometimes produces outward astonishment. Secretly they are probably a little embarrassed for me, and they certainly have a point. But something holds me to this small rectangle of earth on the hill, an attraction that defies any ledger, even an accounting as complex as one's carbon footprint.

As a result, my idea of what passes for a long holiday like Memorial Day weekend has evolved since returning to Oregon. Those three days at the end of May are crunch time in the garden because by then the May sunshine has raised the temperature of the soil, and the warming air carries the promise of more sun in June. Now, on my holiday I do hard time in the dirt.

In the Pacific Northwest we have Murphy's Law of Memorial Weekend: no matter how nice the weather was the first three weeks of May, it will rain over the holiday. This law applies especially to farmers who have managed to mow their hay early and left it to cure in the field exposed to the elements. But on this Saturday, the first morning of the long spring weekend, the weather rules are wrong. I sit on the porch with strong coffee and a notebook, jotting down thoughts and inserting the names of bird songs in the margins of the page: Swainson's Thrush, Black-headed Grosbeak, Steller's Jay. The sun behind me breaches an eastern dam of hills and low morning clouds, becoming a flood of light that inundates the landscape from the top down, hitting first the white-blossomed crowns of apple trees, then spreading over the high ground of the meadow where the garden lies. Flicker, Spotted Towhee, Song Sparrow. The light grows in intensity, pouring downhill into the low-lying areas around the cabin as a House Wren chatters at the oblong opening of a hollow apple tree trunk.

Closing my notebook, I pull on green rubber boots, the right one with a patch over the top where I once impaled myself with a spading fork, and walk up the hill. Annual rye was planted last fall to protect the open ground and now covers the garden beds in a green, two-foot-thick blanket. Power tools have been used only sparingly on the garden since the ground was first broken, and I cut the rye with a machete, gathering the stems into bundles that quickly accumulate into armloads and stack them in a pile outside the gate. The rye will compost and eventually be returned to the soil inside.

The sun climbs and circles to the south, hovering like a large yellow bird over the jumbled fir-covered hills jutting abruptly upward from the opposite side of the valley. I work up the ground with my digging tool, a contraption resembling a spading fork on steroids. From a gardening catalog I figured out some rough dimensions and asked Dad to fabricate this tool for my birthday. The frame is a 24- by 48-inch rectangle of square, tubular steel. Attached to the bottom are five tines, each made from 12 inches of three-quarter-inch-thick round solid steel that has been cut on the ends to a 45-degree angle. The operating instructions for this human powered tiller are simple: stand it upright on the ground, put your full weight on the steel crossbar above the tines and force them completely into the soil, grab the handles at the top for maximum leverage, pull them toward you, then give a shake or a twist to get the upturned earth to break apart. Rest as needed. Drink lots of water. Repeat until the garden bed is completely churned up.

The chocolate-brown earth with bits of green oat stem poking out has an uncomfortable similarity to the logged hillside. A crop is planted, grown, and removed. Animals that have colonized the plants are disrupted. A degree of ruthless control over the land is required. Certainly these two versions of agriculture are different, especially on temporal and spatial scales. The looming starkness of the hillside encompasses several hundred acres of trees that will not regrow to their previous size in my lifetime. In contrast, the garden is 1200 square feet, and within three months it will be covered with head high corn and the broad green leaves of spreading squash vines.

Yet the critical divergence between these forms of agriculture is this: I always tithe to the soil. Every winter I haul in trailer loads of fresh horse manure and straw from my friends the Kimmels, forking it into a huge yellow and green heap outside the east fence. This afternoon the pile is one third its original size, dark brown and crumbly, odorless except for the faint musty smell of various microbes returning all that poop to the earth. Shoveling the compost into a rusty wheelbarrow, I put my hands to the handles, legs directly beneath, and grunt the load around the corner of the fence and through the gate. Six trips, six mounds for one tilled bed. Then I spread and churn it into the top six inches of soil with a spading fork.

A healthy forest needs no such intervention. Forest soils are built over thousands of years by trees that grow, shed their needles and nitrogen-fixing lichens, and then eventually die and rot in place. I find it difficult to imagine that the large scale and repeated removal of Douglas fir, hemlock, and red cedar from what once was a self-regenerating system can do anything but deplete the soil. Immediate losses are obvious; they come from winter rain pelting the bare ground, forming muddy runoff that chokes the waterways below.

Still, I wouldn't have a garden if this land had not at one time been cleared. When digging my beds I occasionally turn up intact pieces of bark and black charcoal left from the trees that were felled and the stumps that were burned two generations ago. In fact, I wouldn't be here to contemplate my sense of place and a healthy relationship to the land if my great-grandparents hadn't been lured from the Midwest by a piece of Oregon/California Railroad Land and the vast forests that fueled a booming timber economy in the last century. Confronting the facts of my family history causes me to pause, wipe my brow, take a deep breath, and exhale some self-righteousness.

The sun slides effortlessly into the western sky, stretching the broken shadow of the large apple tree just outside my south fence downward from the knoll toward Johnny's cabin. No-see-ums begin to bite any patch of exposed skin, so I pull on my long-sleeved work shirt and turn up the collar. The tiny flies still manage to find my ears and a patch of scalp where the back of my hat is open. Two beds have been completed, but there is no more digging left in my arms, legs, or back.

I walk slowly downhill to the pickup. Inside the canopy cover is a plastic grocery bag with five varieties of bean seeds in an assortment of scavenged containers—a cottage cheese carton, a jam jar, some repurposed sandwich bags. The beans all came from Mom, who has diligently grown the plants and saved their seed for many years. They came to her from various sources: Swedish Browns from Grammy; Red Kidneys from cousin Maggie; Tongues of Fire, Yellow-eyeds, and Cannellinis ordered from seed catalogs many winters ago. During the time that Grammy lived with Mom, basketfuls of beans were grown so that Grammy could occupy her winters sitting in the living room shelling seeds from dried pods. The beans occupied her hands, made her feel useful. Now Grammy is gone, and there is talk of Mom and Dad moving to eastern Oregon where the climate is inhospitable to bean growing. Things change and the time has come for the next generation of humans to carry the next generation of beans into the future.

When seeds are saved from plants that have grown for many years in a single place, the plants and the people whom they feed become that place. This plant-human relationship is fundamentally physical. Within a few seasons the genetic makeup of these crops is already being molded by soil and weather and human choice. For Mom's beans, the strongest plants made more of themselves and the largest seeds were selected and planted the following year. When surplus beans are eaten, their proteins are dismantled and recomposed into enzymes that activate the myriad chemical reactions that keep our physical selves running, including the firing of our brain cells that become choices that allow the best beans to persist. So Mom's beans have, in a very direct way, become both her and her place in this bioregion. They will also become part of everyone with whom she shares a handful of seeds, and a simple bean then becomes a fiber in the fabric that binds people to each other and to the land.

I drop beans onto the surface of the two beds, the seeds about four inches apart, marking the boundaries between each variety with upright sticks, methodically pushing the seeds into the fluffy earth with my index finger, smoothing the surface as I go. Now the beans will grow in my hands, a product of Mom's stewardship, a digging tool welded by Dad, the Kimmel horse byproducts, and the peculiar way that the sun, now gliding to roost below the bare western ridge, shines on this ground.

On Sunday two more garden beds were tilled and planted. Now Memorial Day is here, and Murphy finally has his way; the sunshine has been overcome by low clouds and mist, a placid wetness that most Oregonians wouldn't dignify with the label "rain." Dad has organized a work party at the Gunter Cemetery ten miles down the road, the place where my maternal great-grandparents James and Ina Sarah and five of their sons were buried. The old cedar-post fence around the cemetery is falling down. For some reason maintaining this physical boundary demands action, an unwritten family proclamation that all of us were spawned by the people who once stood upright on those bones and raised the people who raised the people who raised us.

So we meet on this misty Memorial Day morning, pulling into the turnout next to the rusty gate and flagpole. Our purpose is worthy of a physically substantive fence, not some half-ass arrangement of mass-manufactured metal posts or namby-pamby prefabricated sections of picket sticks. So Dad has brought on the back of his flatbed pickup a pile of four-inch steel pipes, scavenged from god knows where, to use for posts. He has a portable gasoline generator capable of converting 89-octane fuel into 100 amps of electrical current for running an arc welder that will stick those pipes together into strutted corners across which 13-gauge woven wire livestock fencing can be stretched. He has sacks of concrete and a 55-gallon drum of water and a wheelbarrow and a shovel for mixing the cement that will fix those posts immovably into place in the red dirt. Clearly Dad plans on never doing this project again.

People begin to organize themselves along lines of ability and interest. Dad does the metal cutting and welding. My son Alex enjoys running just the right amount of water into the powdery cement in the wheelbarrow and stirring the gray goop to the consistency of pancake batter for setting posts. Cousin Anne and her husband Dave clear the ever-encroaching salal from around the graves and along the fence line. From the surrounding forest Kim and daughter Laurel dig bleeding heart, their enclosed pink blossoms still nodding over lacy green leaves, and transplant them around the headstones. As is often my custom, I become a free agent, floating from brush cutting to posthole digging to setting posts to stretching new wire, depending on the need of the moment.

We work through the morning and the new fence begins to grow from the side opposite the road. Mom organizes a huge picnic lunch, and we break for sandwiches and potato salad. In the meantime, Anne and Dave's son David arrives with his son Kyle, and the two of them are quickly assimilated into our work party. David is six years younger than I, the offspring of two families whose ancestry traces to the Smith River Valley, and he has spent much of his life hunting and fishing and generally rambling around this area with his father and other relatives.

David has a wonderful memory for history, and much of what he knows about the valley and the people now past pours out of him in a waterfall of words. A grave marked only with a squat iron "T" onto which the inscription "FH 1916" is dribbled crudely in welding bead is for Fred Hardenbrook who lived ten miles down the road: "He was only supposed to be buried here temporarily."

"Last spring Kyle and I caught 35 fish right down there in the creek. We turned 'em all loose."

"Where are all the crawdads we used to see when we were kids?"

"Smith River is dying and I don't know why."

Enough posts have been anchored in the ground to string the wire all the way around, but we will run out of pipe before we can finish the job. Lunch and the exertion of the morning have dulled our sense of urgency, and privately I'm thinking that Dad brought in about the right amount of pipe for today. He shuts down the noisy generator. The silence is momentarily startling. From the truck I bring down several cans of white spray paint and begin covering the rusty pipes that are now posts. The hiss of escaping paint is quickly inhaled by the surrounding woods, and from somewhere deep within myself I unearth the reality that the forest will eventually inhale this cemetery as well. Time and biology are inexorable agents of change, stretching outward into a future we can scarcely imagine.

We must accept that our work today will be undone over the long strand of time, but our efforts are not futile. In the short term the bronze headstones and buried bones will silently resist the amoebic engulfment by industrial timber that has so changed this valley over five decades. The cemetery will remain a family monument, the only Gunter ground left on Smith River except for Johnny's place. But the heart of the matter is this: the cemetery gives us a reason to care, a reason to continue as a tribe, an anchor around which our memory and culture can revolve and remain intact. Today the Gunter Cemetery is for the living.

Returning to the Johnny Gunter cabin, I take up my customary post on the front porch to listen to the land become dark. And to think. A chorus of Swainson's Thrushes calls into the dusk in a series of ascending warbles spiraling upward on invisible evening drafts, interspersed with short tweets rising hopefully at the end. Growing darkness silences the bird songs one at a time, until only a single thrush calls from the black conifers below the cabin.

That odd shiver runs down my spine, energy that is released when everything is right. Although I'm trained as a scientist, I wonder if we place too much stock in science to tell us how we should feel. Seeing a multidimensional landscape reduced to flat barrenness is emotionally jarring. I don't understand why this is so, but I have come to believe that my emotions are worth paying attention to, despite their subjectivity. Do we have some innate template that is a basis for recognizing the tolerances of ecological acceptability? One could speculate that our survival over the vast reaches of history preceding civilization would have depended on such ecological intuition. Or do we resonate with the natural world when it reflects a vibrant state within ourselves? We thrive on depth: deep soil, deep shadows, deep connections to people and places. All of these produce intricate, interwoven, interdependent pieces of our personal ecology. Certainly this much is true: a forest that has been reduced to two dimensions will heal by tending naturally toward complexity.

People heal that way, too.

Epilogue

This afternoon I put the Smith River garden down. Granted, one does not dig a hole out back, lead the garden next to the edge, and shoot it, even though all morning I felt as though I were driving out to put my old horse out of our collective misery. In these parts you kill a garden simply by taking down the deer fence. I was unarmed, so on the way in I stopped at Jerry and Mar-

tha's and borrowed a fence post puller, and stopped inside the Johnny Gunter cabin for a pair of wire pliers.
Even though it was Memorial Day Weekend, it had been
a cold, rain-filled, godforsaken spring and the grass was
still wet, so I had to make a run at the hill. I pulled the
utility trailer into my parking place between the big old
apple tree and the garden gate and got out. I hoped that
the garden didn't suspect what was coming, that it would
never know what hit it. The annual rye I'd planted for
ground cover last fall was a foot and half high, with pale
green seed heads beginning to ripen and nod over. Vol-
unteer kale that had fed me all winter were four feet tall
and sporting clusters of small, bright yellow flowers.
Bindweed, the damned bindweed that was always sneaking under the fence like a stray cat in heat, had made it
inside and was happily flowering too. This afternoon
digging it out would be as useful as picking fleas off the
old horse.

Gray clouds swirled in from the west, dropping
heavy mist while I traveled from post to post using the
pliers to remove the clips that had held the eight-foot
woven wire fence in place, the thin barrier protecting the
garden from protracted death by grazing. I jacked the
red metal posts out of the wet ground and clanged them
into the trailer. Grabbing the fencing, I heaved back-
wards, pulling it loose from the grass and knapweed that
over the years had grown tightly around the bottom,
then gathered it into an eight-foot-long cylinder and bar-
rel-rolled it across the meadow to the barn. No boundaries now existed between the garden and the wild world
outside, no more reason for me to mow and till and fer-
tilize and plant and weed and water and harvest. The
deer and elk would have their way with it.

You see, the garden was never mine, at least in the narrowest sense of possession. When the logging company next door had come to take their trees out, they surveyed the property line. Come to find out, my garden was on their side of the line. They were nice about it—said I could keep gardening there as long as I liked. But after clearcutting the hillside they planted the meadow to Douglas fir seedlings. That's what logging companies do—they plant, grow, and cut down Douglas fir.

Unfortunately they also spray herbicides over the landscape, presumably toward one end—to grow more fir trees faster. So a sea of chemicals now surrounded my garden. This isn't just a figment of my overstimulated imagination; the meadow is turning browner by the day except for the 30- x 45-foot parcel that was not sprayed because they were nice to me and spared my garden.

But there are no islands, not in this meadow, not anywhere. My garden beds have damp spots where water has percolated up through the soil from somewhere nearby, and all the surrounding ground has now been bathed in herbicides. The chemicals will wash off the meadow and hillside into the little creek where torrent and giant salamanders live, and the creek will carry the stuff through the culvert under the road and into the marsh in the valley bottom where chorus frogs breed, and the marsh water will seep into Smith River where orange crawdads crawl and baby Coho swim.

There are no islands. Yet surveyors walk the land with the gadgets of their trade—sextant, compass, clinometer, theodolite—sighting imaginary lines, pissing out make-believe corners with stakes and gaudy colored plastic tape. The surveyors write numbers on a piece of paper describing this fantasy. Then somebody somewhere finds some money, probably not even their own, and purchases that little piece of paper, and the fantasy of ownership continues with rights and privileges that may or may not have anything to do with the connectivity of the biosphere. The surveyor's sextant is agnostic to even the most straightforward of realities, such as gravity and flowing water, never mind the shifting complexities of southwesterly storm winds and sunshine and shadows where calypso orchids bloom and the way in which baby salmon hide.

Nevertheless, this afternoon I gave a nod and a bow to the imaginary lines of ownership. I can't grow my food in a place surrounded by plant poisons that the people who own that property have every legal right to spray. From now on, the Smith River Memorial Garden will be only that—a memory.

BLACKBERRIES IN JULY

To me the Midwest always seemed meteorologically well behaved. Yes, there were the occasional tantrums: spring tornados, summer thunderstorms, and winter blizzards. But the seasons were clearly demarcated and toed the line with astronomical designations of equinoxes and solstices. Now that I'm back in Oregon to stay, it will take nine strong men and a very mean dog to get me out of here again. But living in the Pacific Northwest requires vast amounts of patience with the weather, especially seasonal changes. These occur with little respect for dates on a calendar and behave like a foot-dragging child, never ready to get out of bed or catch the bus or come in for dinner or go to bed. They are nearly always late. The recalcitrant rains of winter have a very strong personality, often refusing to acknowledge the existence of spring, and occasionally they force the issue even into early summer. Although the behavior of the rain verges on that of a spoiled brat, we Oregonians have chosen to live with it, so that when "summer" arrives we leave our raincoats on a hook by the door until at least the Fourth of July.

One morning in early summer when the weather looked a lot like winter, I was driving the scenic back way to the Johnny Gunter place, winding through the

Coast Range west of Lorane. By now this had become my usual route. I've discovered that rolling over the sinuous road through the mountains makes me feel like a participant in the landscape, and for this intimacy I am willing to sacrifice 15 minutes of travel time and steer clear of the impersonal detachment of Interstate 5.

Turning onto a Bureau of Land Management logging road, I shifted down and climbed upward onto the ridges between the Siuslaw and Smith River drainages and thought about the day ahead. I knew that enough sun had managed to break through the rainy spring to bring my Smith River garden shoots breaking to the surface. Even on a dreary morning like this one the usual summer drought loomed in the near future, and some sort of irrigation needed to be installed. Mom and Dad would be at the cabin to mow the grass growing rampantly in the yard and orchard. All things considered, it was a good day to visit. Yet my reasons for going were really only excuses that bobbed along on the surface of things, carried by strong unseen currents.

The gloomy weather and my mood were well matched. Heavy overcast held the shadowy forests of Douglas fir and hemlock close against the mountains. On a sunny day the thimbleberry bushes and vine maples would have flowed together along the roadside in twin streams of bright green, but this morning they seemed the color of overcooked peas, subdued, in slow motion.

This morning I was free to drive leisurely through the Coast Range because my teaching job at the local community college was part time. The pay was low and the benefits nil, but I had desperately needed employment because the research money that had brought me back to Oregon was drying up. That grant had been a spring pond full of promise and possibilities. But when the rains finally end in summer, pools not fed by permanent water evaporate. Not long ago I had found myself gasping in the stagnant puddle of my mismanaged career. While the worst of this emotional drought seemed to have passed, I was still a recovering melancholic and needed to watch my step. My friend Cara, one of the few people I still know from kindergarten days, had recently given me a very sound piece of advice: find some joy every day. Simple wisdom, but I was long overdue for a deposit in my bliss bank.

On the top of the ridge, my plodding existentialist angst was eventually overcome by a blaring message from my bladder that the time had come to stop and enrich the local nitrogen cycle. Reluctantly I slid my foot to the brake pedal, bringing the car to a crunching halt at the gravel intersection of five logging roads. Stopping is a rare event for me, usually reserved for pressing biological needs. Generally these involuntary interludes are an inconvenience, although they have led to some unexpected and seemingly coincidental outcomes; chanterelles, deer, wildflowers, and waterfowl have caught me in various stages of undress. Of course my bodily functions have nothing to do with these fortunate encounters beyond forcing me to pause in my reckless tumble through life so that the world can stand upright and still. Things then come into sharper focus.

This enforced version of Zen worked this morning. I was alone and wandered to the edge of the isolated road, pretending to be looking for something. From the chaotic undergrowth, a wild blackberry bush had sent an exploratory tendril onto the shoulder, where it basked like a thin green snake. A dozen multicolored berries glowed in the subdued light, most of them pie-cherry red and tart enough to pull my cheeks into a permanent pucker. But four were dark purple, tinged with wine, just barely ripe. A small warm flash that accompanies unexpected good luck radiated from the center of my chest. Without thinking I picked the ripe berries, popped all of them into my mouth, and bit down.

My head filled with tart, musky blackberry essence that quickly became a time machine carrying me back through the decades to a logged-over hillside on a sunny July day. Mom and Grammy were blackberry picking from prickly, bejeweled vines cascading over large stumps. My brothers and I were very young and were completely absorbed in blackberry eating rather than filling a bucket for later. There must have been enough berries for everyone, because in the evening a warm pie cooled on the kitchen counter, purple juice oozing from a sugar-speckled crust. Mom spent the next several days probing her berry-stained fingers with a needle trying to remove the tiny, nearly invisible thorns. Blackberry picking can have unforeseen consequences.

My four small blackberries came from a vine deeply rooted in these hills. Grammy's yearly goal was to find enough berries for a pie by the Fourth of July, a daunting task because wild blackberries peak later in the month. This sacrament of early summer likely goes back another generation, when my great-grandparents settled in the upper Smith River Valley.

Since the arrival of my ancestors in the Coast Range near the close of the 19th century, the blackberry flora of the Pacific Northwest has changed dramatically. The Coast Range in those days had only one species with any significance as a food resource, an endemic that I grew up calling the wild blackberry, also more romantically named the dewberry. But in 1885 the mustachioed horticulturist Luther Burbank imported the so-called "Himalaya" blackberry to North America, and it has now happily colonized every open space not covered by concrete or asphalt. Burbank is somewhat infamous for his shoddy record keeping, and botanists would later find that his "Himalaya" blackberry had actually been exported to Germany from Armenia before Burbank got hold of it.

Burbank would never have guessed that the Armenian blackberry would become so pervasively dominant in the western United States or that it would eventually erase the cultural traces of our native Pacific Northwest blackberry. Here in the 21st century if you ask the majority of folks about blackberries they will undoubtedly describe the Armenian newcomer rather than the native wild blackberry. To be fair, Armenian blackberries have a lot to offer, even for a weed. The fruit is spectacularly large, profuse, and juicy. When they ripen in August I can fill a five-gallon bucket in a couple of hours by bicycling to the nearest back alley. In contrast, the petite wild blackberry is a shy denizen of forest glades, with slender vines and small thorns. The berries reach peak ripeness in mid to late July, with fruit about a quarter of the size of their Armenian cousins. One as large as the last joint of your pinky is a real trophy.

In July it's easy to tell when you are in the presence of blackberry consciousness. Just mention that your weekend plans include some blackberry picking and watch the response. Most people will be embarrassed for you, kick the dirt and say, "It's a little early, isn't it?" But those who know will look you in the eye, recognize a fellow native blackberry seeker, then just nod and say nothing at all. They understand that wild blackberry picking is for sentimental fools, poetic vagabonds willing to discard common sense to spend a summer day wandering twisting mountain byways in a freewheeling exploration of the essence of things. They also understand that a fruit-laden patch of wild blackberries is a secret worth keeping.

Normally I'm more of a pragmatist. But a haze of blackberry perfume from those four berries had now permeated every cranny of my brain, displacing worry, anchoring me in a present that was also my past. Climbing back into the car after my impromptu rest stop, I continued driving toward Smith River. The narrow pavement was a black ledge hung from a vertical wall of brown sandstone above a precipitous drop into dense summer foliage. Foxglove was in peak bloom, three feet tall and sporting tubular pink flowers. I had no expectation that the day would lead to anything more than a mouthful of berries and childhood remembrances. Four wild blackberries do not make a pie, and besides … I had eaten them.

But there *were* more berries. They were scattered along the roadside in small patches, and I soon learned that by driving very slowly with the window down I could spot them. Briefly I wondered how long it would take me to cross the United States at this speed, window open, peering along the edge of the road for blackberry-sized objects. Then gray sky closed in, gliding so low over the mountains that its gauzy robe caught on the ridge tops as it passed, leaving ragged pieces clinging to the tallest trees, and a light mist began to fall that gradually became a drenching drizzle. Lunchtime was two hours away, but I ate my sandwich anyway to free the container for the berries that seemed destined to fill it.

Time gradually disappeared until there was only the car and the road, wound inextricably together like music and musician in a meandering melody punctuated intermittently by blackberry breaks. My failures, doubts, and false expectations of myself faded into some quiet, mist-filled canyon in my mind. I began to hope; perhaps there were enough blackberries along the next six miles of road to make a pie. A nine-incher would require four cups.

After an hour and a half the sandwich container was heaping full, and in my generous estimate there were two cups of berries. Hope grew to expectation with each successful stop, and I finally surrendered completely to the process. All I needed was time, and today the hours had become limitless. Because lunchtime was by now legitimately close, I decided to eat a piece of chocolate cake that was taking up valuable space in a quart-size freezer bag and began filling that with berries, too. Over the course of the morning I had discovered that ripe blackberries were found only along the shoulder of the road. This pattern was so predictable that I had developed the half-baked hypothesis that on sunny spring days the pavement absorbed more heat, radiating it back to the surrounding air, creating a slightly warmer microclimate. This microcosm of global warming had accelerated the wild blackberry season by a week or two.

Even in the face of pavement-induced climate change, ripe berries were in extremely short supply. Scarcity often gives birth to frugality. I skimped on taste testing, and in lieu of eating my hard-won fruit I periodically waved purple-stained fingers under my nose, sending that blackberry bouquet floating through my brain and setting my pleasure centers firing like the rapid thumping of a drumming grouse. Chemistry was never my strong suit, and I don't know what sort of aromatic compounds give blackberries their distinctive nose. Whatever they are, wild blackberries have concentrated this essence into a very small package.

That blackberry scent coalesced into a pie that seared itself into my imagination, and I became driven by the vision of it, picking every berry with any prospect of adding to that steamy purple filling: barely ripe, partially fermented, tiny, large, or half-eaten by chipmunks. Surely this mix would give my pie what the wine folks call "complexity." Speaking out loud, I promised the animals that I would leave some. But talk was cheap, and I searched for every dropped berry as if I had lost my wedding ring.

The rain subsided and sunlight burned slowly through the vapor. Parking at a turnout above the three-mile downgrade toward Upper Smith River Road, I discovered that here, for reasons known only to the blackberries, they were especially plentiful. I became a delirious bear, weaving from one side of the road to the other, popping berries into my freezer bag. The return to my car provided a slightly different view, revealing a few more berries. Back at the turnout and giddy with success, I allowed myself to take serious stock of the situation. Opening the rear door I placed the bulging freezer bag next to the heaping sandwich container. There was no doubt; I had enough berries for one unadulterated wild blackberry pie.

Twisting downhill, the road ducked into dark timber, emerging along the sunny edge of a recent clearcut. I spotted no berries along this stretch, perhaps because now that my pie quota had been reached I wasn't looking as carefully. I traveled the last four miles to the Johnny Gunter place without stopping. In three hours I'd driven seven miles.

The driveway gate was open. Pulling through, I parked at the old cabin, amazed to find Mom and Dad still there. Mom became really excited when I showed her the berries, and she began rummaging around to find some larger, more acceptable containers. Burglars had raided the cabin five years ago, so we don't keep anything of value there, but Mom eventually found some margarine tubs, and I happily emptied the contents of my freezer bag and the too-full sandwich container. The berries tumbled in and I dribbled all the remaining juice in after them.

By now the sunlight had searched out blue velvet-lined spaces between white clouds, a perfectly behaved early summer afternoon, so the three of us crowded into my car and headed out for more picking. We drove down Smith River and found another paved logging road to forage along. We found berries there, too, but after only an hour or so the first signs of blackberry fatigue began to seep in, a pleasant boredom reminding me that I really can get enough, even of a very good thing. Returning to the house, Mom and Dad gave me all their berries and wouldn't take any of mine. I telephoned Kim, told her about my day, and explained that at my current average speed I would be home around five. Tomorrow morning.

Reversing course, the car and I found our leisurely way back to town. The intensity of the morning subsided, giving way to deep relaxation. Warmth from the late afternoon sun sent puddles of rain spiraling upward off the serpentine road in strands of silver-gray steam that I imagined rising from the slits of a blackberry pie just pulled from the oven. From a shady, sheltered, fern-filled hollow deep within me, a feeling began to emerge like clear water issuing from a quiet spring, gurgling downhill into full sunlight to become a bright, fully formed stream of truth. The truth is that I am lucky to know blackberries. The truth is that blackberry picking is another transformational ingredient in the crucible of my personal alchemy. The truth is that I began to feel the first real joy in weeks.

STALKING CONSCIOUSNESS

He is heat and light,
beyond thought.
Press your ear to his heart,
feel his scorching blood,
the shimmering fire
coursing wildly from the
Soul of the Earth.

I met the huge buck as day was born. A pool of blood-red light spread slowly toward me from the east, washing away the predawn stars, silhouetting him at the top of a grassy ridge where he walked single file with ten other bucks. The deer were over a mile away and looked tiny in my binoculars, yet even at that distance the buck's great antlers dwarfed those of his companions. Then he strolled off the skyline and vanished into the arid land-scape, a desert wraith with no apparent substance be-yond that which I had given him in my mind.

The vastness separating me from the big buck and my general inclination to hunt animals for meat rather than antlers led me to put his image aside, and I set about searching for deer closer to my overlook. Below me was a basin sparsely covered in September-brown grass, gray sagebrush, the occasional green splash of a juniper tree, with outcrops of burnt orange basalt breaking through as though the land were baring pieces of its soul. A small artery of spring-fed water pulsed from the heart of the high hills behind me, coursing gently across the parched landscape, the rattle of its small riffles nearly silenced by distance and the early morning breeze in my ears.

Further west rose the Cascade Range, a north-south chain of 10,000-foot volcanoes. These are merciless rain killers, capturing eastbound storms and squeezing them until they whimper and die on lava-strewn slopes. Only the strongest tempests muscle into the eastern two-thirds of Oregon, and they arrive severely weakened and wrung out. Thick rainforests west of the Cascades are replaced by a semi-arid steppe where plants grow sparsely and only in places where sufficient moisture and their peculiar adaptations to aridity intersect.

Few humans are attracted to the stark, two-dimensional beauty, and I had spoken to no one other than myself for three days. The space between the first sunset and darkness was the hardest. That evening the dusky stillness became a traitorous jailor stealing through my innermost dungeons, keys rattling as he released the captives that I held there. I knew they were loose, saw their shadowy forms in the window, heard their murmuring as they waited for full nightfall before emerging. Then I had slept, and by morning the gray ones were gone, to where I can't say.

This sagebrush country is not my native habitat. But here there is clarity. From this vantage point I see that I am a hunter, but not necessarily a killer. I pursue animals to become a fully participating predator, completely responsible for the meat that I eat. Killing for antlers seems in conflict with this ideal, although big deer certainly carry more venison than small deer. My ideals also include hunting with traditional archery gear; a long bow that bends only because of the strength that I apply to it, without sights or mechanical assistance from a complicated set of pulleys. Because I have chosen this place on the low end of the continuum of hunting technology, I must find a way to get within 20 yards of an animal with a long evolutionary history and a lifetime of experience in avoiding large predators. This task is so difficult that it doesn't allow me to be picky.

A mile beyond my perch, the creek dribbled past an irrigated alfalfa field, deep green and verdant. In summer the pasture supports a healthy population of deer. They work the graveyard shift, moving out of the surrounding hills in the evening to spend the night tanking up on the moisture-laden, high-protein food. Just before daybreak they begin browsing their way up the draws, returning to the basin directly below me. By midmorning, well-fed and watered, the deer find a room with a view: a comfortable bed under the shade of a juniper tree with a vantage point, much like the one I now inhabit, from which they can scan for predators. They nap and chew their cud through the heat of the day, then in the evening they reverse course and move back into the alfalfa. Methodical as shift workers, they often bed in the same places for many days at a time. When deer find something that works, they stick with it.

Their predictable behavior has adaptive merit in the desert. Like most animals, the deer's job is to eat without being eaten, preferably at night when the dehydrating effects of summer heat are minimized. But this monotonous dependability also can be their undoing; predators see patterns and can use these daily rhythms to their advantage. Humans are particularly adept at pattern recognition. I've been hunting this basin for years now and have developed a good sense of how and when the deer move and where they stop to bed.

Yet deep chasms separate pattern recognition from the knowledge and effort required to put high-quality protein in the larder. My brother's friend Mick helped me bridge that gap. High strung and funny as hell, he was absolutely driven to hunt desert mule deer with archery tackle. He also had a huge heart and would teach anyone the tools of his obscure obsession, if they had the gumption to keep up with him. Mick departed this world in a single-car accident some years ago. But before he left, he showed me some things about bow hunting in these daunting places where no one else would ever try. The concept is straightforward: spot a buck before he spots you, keep track of him until he beds for his daytime snooze, then sneak to within arrow range. This conceptual simplicity completely belies the intricate planning, emotional outlay, and physical effort required by the actual process. Some folks call this land the High Desert; for me, it demands an extremely low profile.

Endless noon heat spread downward from an infinitely blue sky, an oven of desiccating air that sent my sweat immediately airborne. Here, dehydration is a stealthy, relentless stalker. Finding no huntable deer from my perch on the hill, I descended into the shimmering sagebrush of the basin floor, making my way up the opposing hillside. I wasn't hunting *per se*, just traveling to another place for a look at the land from a different angle.

Put simply, I wasn't paying attention. The huge buck rose from beneath a small juniper about seventy-five yards away, lumbered another seventy-five yards, then stopped broadside to look me over, well beyond the range of my longbow. His antlers were heavy and dark, with beams jutting horizontally beyond the ends of his large ears. Flat tines jabbed upward for about eighteen inches. He shambled around the sagebrush-covered hillside, summer fat jiggling under gray hide, and was gone. Placing my hand over my heart, I gave silent tribute to his magnificence. This brand of hunting requires seeing before being seen, and I expected never to encounter him again.

Moving slowly through the sagebrush, I used the binoculars to glass ahead under every juniper, looking for a sign of emerging antlers that would give away the presence of a buck. In an hour I had traveled only 400 yards and looked under every tree large enough to shield a bedded deer from the sun. Finally taking my cue from the animals, I crawled under the sprawling shade of the last juniper, drank my remaining water, and began glassing the opposite hillside. Glistening heat waves danced upward, spirits flickering in the waterless air, daring me to join them. A juniper half a mile away sheltered six does and yearlings, some watching, others with ears back, asleep. In this area, deer without antlers are not human quarry. I scanned slowly to the right for about 600 yards; a single deer materialized under a small tree near the ridge top. Antlers came into focus, and I realized that it was the big buck.

Astonishment quickly gave way to planning. My first move would be to the left, dropping through a small draw that would take me below the edge of the basin and out of sight. Then I would climb to a point well above all of the bedded deer, turn right, then reenter the basin and traverse the hillside to a point directly above the buck. This route would allow me to stay out of sight and downwind from all of the animals that I could see, and I wouldn't blow my cover by spooking the does and yearlings. All of this maneuvering would put me in position for a final sneak on the buck that would be downhill through a crosswind. This was the big picture. Final details would be handled moment by moment.

I descended the draw, left the basin, and panted up the hill in the afternoon heat. My water was long gone. Struggling to contain and focus my nervous energy, I tried to visualize that last moment when the bow would be drawn and an arrow released. My emotions were a clear indication that the hard-edged biological relationship between predator and prey has become convoluted for humans. Subsistence hunters incorporate hunting and killing into their tribal ethos because the survival of the group depends upon it. But in domesticated humans, hunting has become biologically superfluous, and the ritual has been gentrified as "sport." Sport generally implies some form of contest, and the plethora of antler-based record books, big buck prizes, and dead animals hanging from walls are a testament to the competitive aspect of contemporary hunting. Many non-hunters have told me that going into nature with a weapon and lethal intent can't possibly be considered a sport. They are probably right.

Amid the swirling ethical debate one fact seems un-assailable: every person walking the planet kills animals. A shopper leaving the supermarket with a package of pork chops participates, albeit indirectly, in killing a pig. For a short time I was a vegetarian. There are many good reasons for being a vegetarian, but I wasn't off the hook, because horticulture destroys vast numbers of animals on scales ranging from locally microscopic to globally gargantuan. All of this death is invisible to the final consumer and therefore provides a level of what some would call "plausible deniability." If my stalk succeeds, the primary difference between my non-hunting acquaintances and me will be that I have been directly responsible for taking the life of an animal that feeds me.

But in the real world the end of one life is the continuation of another, and participatory eating is a life-giving process. Hunting with archery tackle requires months of preseason preparation and practice. A single stalk may take hours. Processing meat takes even more time, and I do my own cutting and wrapping rather than relying on a butcher. My goal is to be so completely invested in all aspects of the experience that in the end a package of venison becomes a conduit connecting me intimately with the land: the quiet chill of predawn, untamed animals, physical toil, and lonely sunsets. Although I've accepted hunting as a responsible, life-affirming way to eat, paradoxically I have not made my peace with killing. I hope I never do.

My direct participation took me to the meager shade of a small juniper perhaps seventy yards above the bedded buck. Carefully I shed my gear bag and boots; the final crawl would be done in stocking feet. Carrying my bow, two arrows, and binoculars, I began in a crouch, moving cautiously from bush to bush, making my way down the gentle slope of the hill. A stiff breeze blew steadily against the point of my left shoulder, occasionally shifting over to my shoulder blade, threatening to strand me upwind of that exquisitely sensitive nose.

The distance closed. At forty yards I was on my belly, a piece of grilling meat sizzling between two layers of heat, one radiating from the ground, the other from the sun overhead. Pulling one knee and the opposite elbow forward, I hitched ahead like an ungainly lizard. Six inches from my face, beautiful pebbles born in the ancient inferno of volcanoes and flood basalts littered my path: brown, beige, red, and white. Occasionally I rose just high enough to catch a glimpse of those remarkable flat-tined antlers. The buck was still in his bed.

I began to focus on the wind. When it blew more strongly I used the covering sound to move ahead, carefully removing from my path any twig that might snap and give me away. When the breeze died back I became still as a corpse, unwilling to risk with any noise all that had been gained. My desiccated brain felt as though it had shriveled into a raisin. I arrived behind the last sagebrush, less than twenty yards from the buck. His dark antlers rocked gently as he chewed his cud. He had no clue I was there.

Then a remarkable thing happened. Perhaps it was the beginning of heat exhaustion or maybe the unravelling of emotions strung too taut for too long. Carefully I rolled onto my back. As I lay there, a spontaneous grin cracked across my chapped face. It was a smile of recognition; unwittingly I had crawled into the holy grail of meditation. I had become completely alive, one hundred percent committed to the intensity of the moment. In this place there were no deadlines, no bills to pay, no people to please, no depression, no future or past. Time didn't stop; it utterly ceased to exist. There was only sun and wind and hot dirt and sore knees and the feel of my heart driving overheated blood thickened by dehydration and laced with adrenalin from one end of my prone body to the other. To be so lost in that instant may be the closest thing to immortality that I have achieved in this life.

An arrow was nocked and ready. I rolled back to my stomach, inhaled deeply, then simultaneously rose to my knees and drew the bow. The buck's excellent peripheral vision served him well, and he spotted me immediately. Dry twigs crunched as he rose and stood broadside for perhaps two seconds, staring, wide antlers framing the sweep of tawny grass and olive sage in the basin below. The string was loosed, its twang slightly muffled as it brushed against my shirtsleeve near the end of its cast. The green shaft glided with deadly grace above sun-burned grass, red feathers twirling gently, guiding a razor-sharp broadhead toward that point immediately behind the buck's shoulder where his Achillean secret of heart and lungs lay shielded by thin ribs. At the last lethal moment, the energy lost to the arrow when the bowstring had ticked my shirtsleeve caused the trajectory of the shaft to drop off. The broadhead passed a harmless hair's breadth below the buck's brisket. He trotted about 100 yards across the hill to my left, stopping by a juniper to watch me.

"Go, you old son-of-a-bitch," I quietly rasped.

He stood for a moment longer. Some signal seemed to pass between us. Then he ambled over the hill, to hang forever on the walls of my memory.

THE MEMORY TREE

Our phone was ringing at 6:30 on a September morning. At that hour a ringing phone is either the wrong number or bad news. Kim was immediately out of bed to answer, and through my grogginess I realized that she was up quickly because she hadn't been asleep. Yesterday her instinct had told her that this call was coming, and last night she had been in a deep funk, an unusual mood for her. She has a kind of telepathy for such things, a deep intuitive core that serves notice of major rifts in her personal universe. Her voice broke slightly as she handed me the phone. "It's your mom; I think you'd better talk to her."

Mom was mostly matter of fact. "Grammy died last night."

Our conversation was short and business-like. Mom still needed to call her brother and sisters, the beginning of a loosely structured phone tree beginning with the closest relatives and eventually encompassing the vast expanse of Grammy's family. This was news that was not news. Grammy's health had been failing for several years now, and she could have left us at any time. She made it to age 99 because of a stubborn streak that ran so deep and wide that she was unwilling to yield to anything, even to the inevitable that trumps all of the inevitables.

My parents had borne the lion's share of Grammy's elder care. Her declining memory first became apparent when one day she called Mom to ask how to make sauerkraut, a question akin to Henry Aaron asking how to swing a bat. Grammy eventually came to live with Mom and Dad, and until last night this had been a 365-day-a-year job sustained by their staunch commitment that she would spend her last years surrounded by people who loved her rather than uniform-clad attendants.

The funeral was standing room only. A person can touch a lot of people after living 99 years anchored to their place, where family is everything and you've had seven kids, most of them with kids, plenty of those with kids, and even a few of those with kids. Several of us spoke at the service, and I unexpectedly found myself choking on emotion.

On Saturday following the funeral my spirit felt dried up and malnourished. I was longing for a trip to the old family place at Gunter, as though I needed to regrow some severed roots. In late summer the Willamette Valley begins to take on the color of a baking cheesecake; Oregon ash trees overflow with warm sunshine, and surplus yellow oozes ever so slightly from green leaves. But on this Saturday, the morning was unusually gray, a hint that the summer drought may have been ending. Kim and I packed raincoats and lunch and piled Alex and Laurel into the car. We took the freeway route, eventually finding our way to Upper Smith River Road, then following the headwaters of Smith River where pavement and creek twist together like mating snakes, winding through Douglas fir forests and golden grass. The road is motion sickness waiting only for the right time and person, and Alex was that person. We stopped so that he could move to the front seat.

From a deep pool of memories I reeled up a trip over that road from my distant past. It was the day before Christmas, I was five years old, and the Christmas Eve celebration was to be an extended family party at Grammy and Grandpa Roy's house at Gunter. Grandpa Roy was Grammy's second husband, the only maternal grandfather I had known. He loved his step-grandchildren and probably spoiled us horribly. In those days Upper Smith River Road was gravel, and to a young boy the trip seemed an eternity. Mom had gone ahead of us with her older sister Zelma, carrying with her my three-month-old youngest brother Todd. Dad followed later with my other two younger brothers and me in the blue Rambler station wagon. We pulled into the parking area in front of the gray, two-story Gunter house, then mysteriously left without getting out of the car. Dad turned to the three of us in the back seat.

"Your Grandpa Roy passed away."

I thought that I knew what he meant. But euphemisms don't work well on five-year-olds, and I decided to try denial.

"You mean he passed out?"

More silence.

"He had a heart attack and died."

Roy had been in the kitchen mixing his family-famous Tom and Jerry batter when his life simply and abruptly ended. We drove to my Aunt Thelma's place two miles upstream from Gunter. I remember the living room, the circle of relatives, Grammy's face red from crying, my cousin Richard admonishing me to give

Grammy a hug. There was no getting around it; Grandpa Roy was gone, suddenly and with absolute finality. I don't remember grieving; probably I processed his death in the way five-year-olds deal with such things and simply got on with the business of living.

Grammy was born and raised at Gunter, but with Grandpa Roy's passing her time there ended with the same story retold a million times across rural America: kids grew up, parents grew old, the place grew too big to keep up, medical care was too far away, and it was best to move into town. So eighty years of continuity were broken, and Grammy came to Eugene. I can only imagine how wrenchingly hard it must have been for her. But she was a practical woman. Kim and I visited Grammy regularly after our return to Oregon. By then she was living with Mom and Dad, her brain honeycombed by dementia. Her parting words often were "Come visit me anytime. I live in the house on the hill between two creeks."

Haney Creek and Panther Creek flow southward out of parallel canyons, entering Smith River about a quarter mile apart. Together these three streams enclose a large flat with deep, flood plain soil. A small knoll overlooks the flat. Grammy and Grandpa Roy's house was still standing on that hill when Kim and I visited 25 years ago. But by then it was nothing but a hollowed-out shell; the first floor was being used by a herd of feral cattle that roamed the valley. The place was bulldozed and burned two years later. I suppose a sort of euthanasia was in order; better the fuzzy memories of childhood than a house full of cow manure.

By the time we parked at the base of the knoll, Alex was feeling better. We found the unused driveway now overgrown with Scotch Broom and walked up to the burned-out foundation. Cracked and crumbling concrete was surrounded by a mongrel plant community composed of unkempt ornamentals and native shrubs. I could feel the disequilibrium of a landscape in flux. When people leave, the first things to go are the inanimate vestiges of humanity: the house, fences, and goldfish pond. These have no energy of their own beyond their creation and maintenance by people who once lived there. Introduced plants persist longer because they maintain themselves by their own photosynthetic effort. However, in the absence of human initiative and sweat all of these interlopers will yield to relentless reclamation by wild nature, to the plants that have always grown here: hazelnut, hawthorn, dogwood, and Douglas fir. These organisms have had the signature of this place drafted into their genetic architecture over millennia.

We stood on the overgrown knoll looking through an open space downhill to the west, across the flat toward Haney Creek. More fragments of memory floated by like leaves in a lazy summer stream: little kid anxiety when I was dropped off for a long visit, milking, feeding pigs, haying, digging fishing worms out of the manure pile with cousin Frank. I pointed out to my family the barn and garden that had once stood at the base of the hill, now visible only to me, only in my mind. Kim cared because I cared. Alex and Laurel were half-listening, and who could blame them? Their personal histories were still short, their world still in the moment, and to them the scene below us was only a meadow mostly covered with brush.

The old orchard rose above the Scotch Broom and blackberries, a tangible anchor securing the hazy memories of early childhood to the immediacy of the September morning. There was the sharp cry of Steller's Jays, the pungent aroma of overripe blackberries and drought-scorched grass still wet from last night's mist. We followed a track off the hill and wandered through one-hundred-year-old apple trees still standing watch over the meadow.

Some trees were three stories tall, their limbs festooned with unripe apples. Their aged and unkempt arms seemed to reach down to me, grateful for my return. I wanted to trim their broken branches, prune off the suckers growing like wild hair, and provide them some vestige of their former dignity. They deserved this because they were raised well. As young saplings the single stem that grew hell-bent-for-leather skyward was "headed off" to produce three or four main branches. These were propped at 45-degree angles until they could support their own weight, and they became multiple fruit-bearing trunks growing upward and outward, leaving an open center to let in plenty of light. Perhaps this is the way we should be bringing up our children; what more could we want for them?

We wandered over to the space near where the barn once stood. A large fruit tree grew straight up for perhaps sixty feet. Drawing close, we realized that it was covered with beautiful green pears. Pears are picked green and unripe in September when the fruit is fully formed but not soft and prone to bruising. Within moments I succumbed fully to my foraging impulse. Kim and the kids watched as I jumped and was just able to grab the lowest limb, pulling my legs up and over my head, hooking them around the horizontal branch, hoisting myself into an upright sit. A bear had been there before me, the fresh vertical furrows of her claw marks clearly visible in the trunk amid the countless sapsucker holes.

Climbing upward, I felt the exhilaration of a five-year-old just liberated from the earth. The pears, the *ohmygodIveneverseenanythinglikethese* pears, hung from sagging branches like jade-colored tears. I became a kid on a green jungle gym, hanging by one arm while stretching out with the other to pick one of the pendulous fruits. They were D'Anjous, a winter storage variety, more squat than a Bartlett, with a short, thick neck tipped quizzically to one side. Their light green skin was the texture of emery paper, flawless, without worms or scab despite decades without spraying or fertilizing or pruning of any kind. For a moment I enjoyed the weight in my hand, took in the sensuous shape. Then I tucked my zipper-fronted shirt tightly into my belt and placed the pear gently inside this makeshift marsupial pouch.

Swinging from limbs forty feet up, I filled my shirt with pears while my risk-averse wife stared upward in horrified fascination, probably wondering whether she should shield her children's eyes from this spectacle of reckless behavior. My shirt was soon full and the ground forces were enlisted. Kim positioned herself below an opening in the branches, and I lobbed pears for her to catch. Unfortunately the free-falling fruit gained enough velocity to sting her hands like hard-thrown baseballs. She dropped as many of these gravity assist pitches as she handled, and the misses hit the ground hard. This is the kiss of death for an unripe winter pear because they must be stored to ripen properly, and a bruise usually turns to rot.

Because the tree was so heavy with fruit, I didn't care if we wasted a few pears. The entire enterprise was a spontaneous adventure anyway, and the deer and elk would come in the night to clean up the mess. But Kim felt otherwise. Large, unblemished pears become objects of art for a reason—they are beautiful. So with pioneer ingenuity that would have made my ancestors smile she pulled her jacket from around her waist and held it between outstretched arms, forming a hybrid between an oversize catcher's mitt and a fireman's trampoline, a contraption that brought the accelerating pears gently to earth. The kids were quickly in on the act, and green missiles landed with a muffled "whump" into their outstretched jackets. The technique was refined; they discovered that if they allowed a jacket arm to dangle toward the ground, the rocketing pear could be subdued and allowed to slide down the sleeve and pop out the cuff, landing gently at their feet.

Pears piled up. The sun finally awoke and began to assert itself, running the clouds out of the valley like unwelcome guests who had come early and stayed too long. My foraging mojo was in full flux, and I didn't want to stop. But I wasn't really five years old, at least physically, and grinding fatigue began to dull the polish on my harvest-induced adrenaline. Grudgingly I gave in to middle age and retraced my climb, easing downward out of the tree, using the last of my waning arm strength to drop myself gently to earth from that lowest, barely reachable limb.

We surveyed the pears stacked like green cannon-balls beneath the tree. The shooting was over, and each rotund fruit contributed to a collective question: "Now what?" We had come only to visit, only for memories, and hadn't planned on participating in this rite of harvest, the communion of earth, sun, plants, and people. We had no buckets or baskets or boxes for moving fifty pounds of pears from point of picking to place of consumption. The pears were green but the time was ripe for more innovation. We knotted the arms of our pear decelerators (aka rain jackets), carefully packed each one with fruit, and pulled the zippers closed over the lumpy cargo for the short hike to the car.

That day became a September leaf drifting from an azure sky, falling into a stream of memory as seamless with the present as unblemished pear skin. The old pear tree is thoroughly integrated into the local ecology; its sap feeds sapsuckers, and pollinators are fed by blossoms that mature into fruit that feed elk and bears and people. But this tree has become more than part of a strictly biological network of relationships. The ancient giant has lasted longer than the humans who planted it and is now the sapwood for memory that flows through people in an unbroken stream from roots to leaves. My kids will remember catching falling pears where Grammy used to live, just as I remember the people before me who tended this orchard and literally lived on the fruits of their labor, and they remembered those before them who put those saplings in the ground. Those memories connect us to others who owed their existence to the land, those to whom we also owe our existence. When we look and feel closely, biology and culture become interwoven into an ecology of heritage, the network of biological, cultural, and spiritual relationships that make us cohesive human beings fully integrated with Nature.

We stowed our pears safely in the trunk. I looked back across the flat to the old pear tree. Her leaves were an apron, the limbs were open arms drooping under the load of many years but still strong and productive. She is loyal to those who love her, ready to give what she has, but only after a little effort invested on our part. With some luck she will outlast me, and I can return in the dry days of late summer, clambering like a little kid into his grandmother's lap.

JOHNNY GUNTER'S POTATO

Outside my office window a sun-filled October afternoon glows so close to perfection that it nearly hurts. The air has baked to 75 degrees, dry and clear as high-grade champagne. Autumn afternoons like this don't often visit western Oregon. Late October is when Pacific storms begin to roll inland from the southwest. Through the eyes of a satellite these tempests are beautiful gray pinwheels rotating slowly clockwise. Here on the ground, in the place where people live, where the last crop of tomatoes is being harvested and canned, where winter squash with crinkly green and gray skin are picked and placed carefully in the pantry, blue skies change to leaden overcast and soaking rain wets the lips of a landscape parched by summer drought. Everything changes, even time. Late October is the Falling Back, when our summer Daylight Savings account is emptied and becomes a winter Standard of dark, cold rides home. In late October people stack their wood and refill prescriptions for Prozac. Late October is the beginning of "hunker time."

There will be no hunkering this afternoon. From my window the day may as well have a "Look But Don't Touch" sign on it, so in a temporary fit of complete sanity I fold up the laptop computer and walk out without it, counting my blessings every step of the way that what I do for money allows me to get away with such truancy. Other tasks are waiting that replenish my soul rather than my wallet. Arriving home I change into real work clothes, then throw a shovel, spading fork, and a few buckets into my aging pickup. Together we head southwest out of Eugene, toward the Smith River garden.

Shedding suburbs like layers of clothes, I wind through the familiar back way toward Lorane. Western Oregon is renowned for its greenery, but today yellows dominate the color scheme; a golden sun shines on summer-browned grasses, Oregon ash trees stream along the creek bottoms with leaves bleached nearly blond in the bright light. Stopping briefly at the Lorane General Store, I grab a giant white chocolate–macadamia nut cookie, half-cooked and gooey, exactly the way I like them.

Twisting into the Coast Range, greens regain pre-eminence on the fall palette, with thick stands of young Douglas fir forming a shady corridor through which the road wanders southwest along the ridges. Occasionally I pass some second growth stands old enough to contain an understory of vine maple, my new favorite tree. The delicate spring flowers are an early nectar source for my honeybees. The wood is extremely tough and springy and used by Native Americans for digging sticks, and when burned slowly it makes decent smoked salmon. But in October all of the utilitarian value contained in vine maple is superseded by beauty, when yellow and orange leaves dance like brightly clad elves inside the dark forest.

The first fallen leaves litter the driveway to the Johnny Gunter cabin. I drive past the house and up the gently sloping hill to the garden, where most of the raised beds have been prepared for winter. A groundcover of oats and fava beans is emerging from the chocolate brown earth. In their public life these small plants protect the dirt from an onslaught of winter weeds and rain, but beneath the soil they carry on a more important covert existence. Finely branching roots break up the dense soil and will eventually add nitrogen and compost that foster a dynamic, subterranean ecosystem of earthworms, fungi, and bacteria. I forgot to close the garden gate last weekend, and the oats have contributed to the more charismatic fauna above the ground. Two deer, a doe and her yearling judging by their tracks, have wandered in and cropped off the untapped resource of tender green shoots. No matter; the oats have all winter to grow back.

Despite all the fresh new growth, the exuberance of the summer season has mostly passed, leaving only the lingering warm spot of satisfaction from harvesting boxes of winter squash, potatoes, and corn. In these last beautiful days of autumn the garden and surrounding meadow bask in peaceful anticipation of winter, and in this moment there is no place, no time in which I would rather be. This gives me butterflies.

One small section of garden farthest from the gate has not been planted to groundcover. Here, a group of dark green potato plants has grown continuously since early last spring, lush and luxuriant, some still bearing a few lavender-colored flowers. This indeterminate growth is generally considered aberrant potato behavior. My Yukon Golds, All Blues, and Cranberry Reds have long since flowered and died back. They were harvested in August. Now October is nearly over, and this wacky potato foliage continues to spill onto the garden paths. But this spirited growth will end in a few days with a hard freeze due in from the north, so the time has come to discover what sort of subterranean secret exists beneath these enormous plants.

Getting ready to dig potatoes is like preparing to open a birthday present that has been sitting mysteriously on the front table for five months. Peeling off my shirt, I grab a six-gallon bucket and settle in with the spading fork, turning the earth from well outside each plant to avoid damaging the crop. Potatoes of all shapes and sizes begin burbling to the surface, from classically round to gnarly and grotesque, small nodules to softball-sized leviathans. Their skins are light beige with subdued pink mottling, reminiscent of raspberry swirl cheesecake, and they are dimpled with tiny, pink eyes squinting under the mellowing afternoon sun like a two-day hang-over. Some of the larger tubers have been chewed on by the resident gopher. These potatoes are not the Idaho bakers that fill our supermarket bins, bred and sorted for unblemished uniformity. And unlike those monotonous, plastic-wrapped, godforsaken Russets, these potatoes have a story.

Marion Gunter lived a quarter mile west of younger brother Johnny, just below the knoll where my garden lies. Both men made regular trips from Smith River to the northern California logging town of Happy Camp to visit their youngest brother Don. On one of those trips, Don gave some seed potatoes to Marion, who was not a gardener and passed them along to Johnny. Johnny knew a good food plant when he saw one and immediately began growing the potato. Fortunately he was also a good neighbor and gave some seed tubers to Mrs.

Leslie two miles up the road. Also fortunately, she decided to spread the goodwill and passed some surplus tubers along to Jerry and Martha Gatchell, who then sent some over to Bruce across the road. Over the years, this odd potato had, with the help of its human allies, established several new outposts in the Smith River Valley.

A few years ago Mom and Dad were visiting Bob and Demaris Tronson, who had recently lost their house to fire and been living in an old, donated mobile home. Bob was besieged with heart problems and he and Demaris were moving back to Drain because life in town, even a small town, is more forgiving to older folks with health issues. The Gatchells were also visiting that day, picking up a variety of things that Bob and Demaris would not need in their new digs.

The conversation turned to heirloom fruits and vegetables, and Martha starting talking about the raspberry cheesecake potato. She was a little embarrassed that Mom hadn't heard about it, having always assumed that Mom was up to date on these important aspects of the family legacy. When Jerry's mother Lois died later in the summer, Mom went to the memorial service and Martha and Jerry brought her some tubers for seed. Mom and I have a soft spot for family history of any kind, especially where it pertains to food, so last spring we started growing the potato at the Johnny Gunter place.

No one is certain how Don Gunter came by the potato. The Gatchells sent a few to Ronniger's Potato Farm, a seed potato company in Idaho, who pronounced it unique and marketed it for a time as the Johnny Gunther [sic] Potato. More recently I sent some tubers to Dr. Alvin Mosely, a faculty member in the Oregon State University Department of Crop and Soil Sciences and author of the Potato Information Exchange website. He'd never seen anything like it and suspected that someone may have developed the variety from seed. Most potato propagation is done from tubers that are genetically identical to the plant from which they came. However, some varieties produce seeds in small, tomato-like fruits that can be collected and "grown out." The genetics become complicated because modern potatoes carry four copies of every chromosome, rather than the usual two, and these multiple copies are stirred in unpredictable ways during the genetic reshuffling that occurs when seeds are produced. This genetic mixing can produce a wild array of potato offspring, any one of which could be propagated as a clone by planting their tubers. So one possibility is that Don developed the Johnny Gunter potato from seeds of another variety.

Dr. Mosely is a good scientist and a true devotee to the advancement of potato knowledge. Looking for some solid answers, he sent a few Johnny Gunter potatoes to his colleague Dr. Charles Brown, a potato specialist at the United States Department of Agriculture station in Prosser, Washington. Using methods based on DNA similarity, Dr. Brown discovered that this bizarre-looking spud did not enter the world of potatoes recently and is not closely related to modern strains. Quite the opposite. The Johnny Gunter potato is genetically most similar to several varieties that had a common ancestor in Chile, the world's center for wild potato species. One of those close relatives is the Ozette, a red fingerling potato that, according to Dr. Brown in his article "The Potato of the Makah Nation," was likely introduced into northwestern Washington in 1792 by Spaniards who had established a fort at Neah Bay. The Ozette was quickly adopted by the Makah tribe and is named for one of their villages.

A year later the Johnny Gunter potato story took another turn when I wrote about it for our local natural history society newsletter. Reida Kimmel, one of our members who has supported my gardening habit over the years by providing me with loads of horse manure, buttonholed me at the next meeting and stated in no uncertain terms that she had that potato. She brought me a few in a brown paper bag and I was a little stunned to see the small pink eyes of Johnny Gunter potatoes staring back at me from the bottom of the sack. Reida had received the tuber in 1970 from an elderly couple living on San Juan Island in northwestern Washington who had called it the "Red Indian."

The science, geography, and sociology of this potato fascinate the living daylights out of me. There is a close genetic relationship between the Red Indian/Johnny Gunter and the Ozette, there is geographic proximity between San Juan Island where Reida had received the Red Indian and the Spanish forts where the Ozette was introduced, and there is a tantalizing Native American link in the naming of the Red Indian and the adoption of the Ozette by the Makah. None of these associations prove anything, but the connections are intriguing and provide a framework for future discovery. In the meantime, we can discard the idea that the Johnny Gunter potato was a product of Uncle Don's horticultural experimentation; he was simply a roundabout recipient of a very old potato variety.

Regardless of the details, the genealogical roots of the Johnny Gunter potato illustrate a couple of things I adore about science. People develop ideas about how the world works. Information is then gathered and processed, decisions are made about the original idea, and then we move ahead with matters. Part of this moving ahead is accepting that it is *completely* okay to hurl your brightest ideas at an interesting problem, collect data to the best of your ability, and in the end be wrong about the initial idea. While this lesson in ego control is easy in theory, it can be difficult in practice.

The story line of the Johnny Gunter potato is a bit complicated and untidy and contains too many characters. But that is also the point. The potato owes its existence to untold generations who for centuries have passed it along through an informal network of family and friends. Those of us blessed with a start of these potatoes understand that a spring trip to the local feed-and-seed for more tubers isn't a possibility. The only way to propagate the potato is to grow it, year after year, always leaving a supply for planting and sharing in the spring. This web of human relationships means that more people have it. If a catastrophe strikes and causes one of us to lose our potatoes, we can always get some seed from the neighbors. In the end, the likelihood is lessened that a rare endemic potato variety will go extinct.

The Johnny Gunter potato provides one good reason to stay in touch with the neighbors, but what about its value as a food plant? An intergenerational network of potato growers has propagated a variety with some attractive features. The plants grow the entire summer, and their underground stems produce tubers all season. One outcome of this indeterminate growth is that even in late October there are potatoes in all stages of development, from thick-skinned "hardened off" spuds ready for storage to thin-skinned "new potatoes" that are usually available from standard varieties only in late spring or early summer. The potato seems to have been less attractive to gophers. This year I lost half my tried and true Yukon Gold plants to this subterranean depredation; a single gopher ate them from the roots up, leaving anchorless, pathetically wilted plant corpses sprawling on the surface.

Best of all, the yield of Johnny Gunter potatoes on only thirty square feet of garden bed is becoming impressive, at least in my limited potato growing experience. But at the moment that yield is beginning to take its toll. I thought the harvesting was going to be a fifteen-minute job, but it has stretched to half an hour and I've dug only half the plants. My internal thermostat has long since forgotten how to cope with late summer heat, and I'm sweating profusely in the unseasonable October warmth. My bucket is so full that I'm forced to heap the potatoes carefully over the rim. Five plants remain to be dug, so I swap the topped off bucket for an empty one in the pickup. Starting on a new container always stirs mildly conflicting emotions; I've never quite been able to reconcile the deep satisfaction of a filled bucket with the uncomfortable sense that I'm starting completely over.

Potatoes rattle into the empty pail in ones, twos, and threes, each individual seemingly tuned in to its own private potato-growing program. The tubers are too haphazard in size and shape to be of any commercial value and will never find a home on industrial farms championing crops that are as ecologically and genetically monotonous as waiting in line for an underwear sale. Those crops are manipulated for mass production, herbicide resistance, and "marketable" appearance, and potatoes that can't be sliced into pristine longitudinal fingers for French fries need not apply. This profit driven approach to food has yielded a variety of consequences that are not polite dinner conversation: water from ancient aquifers sucked down faster than a glass of iced tea on a hot day, topsoil silting up streams, poisoning of the remaining soil and water, and the no-holds-barred-take-no-prisoners-get-the-hell-out-and-don't-let-the-door-hit-you-on-the-ass destruction of family farms. The marketing slogan that industrial agriculture is necessary to "feed a hungry world" is now a joke that isn't funny. But many people are snapping out of their zombie state and waking up to the idea that agribusiness is mainly feeding insatiably hungry corporations.

The knobby, pink-eyed, overgrowing Johnny Gunter potato will always stand outside of this shortsighted madness, and this afternoon I couldn't really care less about industrial potato growing. In the syrupy, shirtlessly warm October sun, I want to believe that the small portion of genetic diversity sequestered in this simple potato might somehow save the world. On the surface this is absurd. My garden on the hill doesn't produce enough potatoes to feed even my own family, never mind a neighborhood or small city the size of Eugene. Yet the Johnny Gunter potato contains a universal saving grace: it is a microcosm of the future of farming emphasizing sustainability through soil growth, local food production, and maintenance of genetic diversity by seed saving, a system that places a premium on the sociological, ecological, and genetic continuity of human-plant interactions and local food communities.

The Johnny Gunter potato certainly has horticultural merit, otherwise it would long ago have been relegated to the scrap heap of aborted agricultural experiments. But my Smith River neighbors also keep the potato for its uniqueness and in memory of Johnny, a lifelong inhabitant of the valley. They don't have a mission statement or an electronic discussion group or a website or a Facebook page. They are acting as a very small, localized food community simply by spreading a good thing around, looking after each other, themselves, and their culture. This potato owes its continued existence to their homegrown, hand-me-down approach to agriculture.

I uproot the last potato plant and move it to the compost bin. The second bucket is nearly full. The dry air is cooling rapidly as the silent autumn evening settles in, and I retrieve my shirt that has been hanging from a fence post. My afternoon dies in perfection, pure, immaculate, and unsullied by the monotonous, clonal uniformity of civilization. The roots of the Johnny Gunter potato aren't deep, but they are growing, wending their way through the rich earth of humanity, absorbing nutrients from our collective local culture, anchoring us to our place while feeding the hearts and bellies of all who participate in its continued existence.

CIDER DAY

Years ago when I first suggested that we juice the fall apples in the Johnny Gunter orchard, I didn't know about the old black-and-white photograph. The picture conjures a swirl of emotions, currents rising from hidden places in deep water, gently stretching the surface. Occasionally I feel as if I were born in the wrong age, that I should have lived back then, been there with them. Now and again I want to reach into the picture, put my hand on the men's shoulders, and ask them to tell me what it was like on that day and all their other days. This longing produces a hollow sensation at the base of my throat, as if I were looking at the last picture of an extinct animal. My curiosity mourns their passing; I grieve not so much for the people or the times now gone but for the things they knew that are now permanently lost to me.

Someone loved this photo. It hangs on a hallway wall between Mom and Dad's laundry and family rooms. The varnished 8- by 10-inch maple frame is handmade, and there are nicks from the saw blade inscribed in small arcs in the wood. The backing is a piece of cardboard box onto which Mom has written the names of the three men surrounding a large cider press. A homemade wooden flatbed wheelbarrow is parked to the right. To the left of the press is "Mr. Rennie," a stout fellow in a floppy-brimmed hat and suspendered work pants. His back is turned and his face is only partially profiled, but I sense from the way that he carries himself that he is older. In the center and directly behind the press is Don Gunter, the youngest of the Gunter siblings, who has a shock of dark hair and is dressed in bib overalls and long sleeves. He's looking down at the press and clearly smiling. To the right of the press is another handsome young fellow wearing belted work pants and short sleeves. Smiling broadly, he holds a half-eaten apple in his left hand while gesturing to a cup in his right that must have held apple cider. This is Don's older brother Johnny. Don and Johnny were born near the turn of the 20th century, and in the photograph they are young men probably in their twenties, so the picture was taken sometime in the 1920s.

Here in the full color 21st century, I pull off the road at the top of the ridge, get out, and gaze westward across the green and gold concertina folds of the Coast Range. In the stillness of the October night a mass of clouds gathered over the wrinkled mountains, but morning sunshine is slipping through sideways, opening crevasses of blue light in the iron glacier of overcast. The clouds are slowly and silently giving way to the sun, and in the soft butter light of the new day big leaf maples emerge from hiding, small flash mobs of hand-size yellow leaves waving from fir-clad hillsides. The landscape is a study in schizophrenia; bright and dark, exuberant and subdued, cheerful and solemn, frivolous and deep.

I search the shadowed valleys for the Johnny Gunter cabin, a five-acre postage-stamp place with waiting apple trees, knowing the orchard can't be seen from here. But I can't help myself—I'm always searching, hunting, feeling as though something is misplaced, wondering what that something is or pretending to know. Curiosity gnaws at me constantly, chewing a donut hole in my center that will never be filled. So I search for the sake of searching, because full-on unfettered life is for the curious.

Planting my inquisitive, never-satisfied self back in the pickup, I descend into the dappled creek bottom, cider press in tow. Truck and trailer slice through beams of sunlight slanting between straight gray alder trunks, bending around vine maple leaves that are orange then red now yellow, flashing by in a silent cacophony of color that becomes nearly hallucinogenic. This wild whirling of sun and shadow, fiery leaves and green needles, warm days and cool nights, placid blue skies waiting on churning gray storms combine to create the maniacal, bipolar, butterflies-in-your-stomach experience of autumn in the Northwest.

Pulling into the Johnny Gunter place, the meadow and orchard are in full sunlight. The first drenching fall rains have come and gone, and the thirsty brown grass of summer is green again. Mom and Dad arrived before me, but not by much; they are toting a cooler and bags of lunch food into the cabin. Kim, Alex, and Laurel are somewhere behind us, I'm not sure how far. The kids are at an age where they would rather sleep than make cider. Because we needed two vehicles to transport everyone anyway, Kim and I had decided that family harmony could best be maintained if she delayed her departure and did the patient cajoling. I took the easy way out and left early to meet Mom and Dad to start picking apples.

Dad and I unload our small cider press and set it up in front of the cabin. The components of our press are roughly the same and assembled similarly to those of the old behemoth in the photograph, but this modern version is smaller, lighter, and more portable. Our press is also considerably less charming. The frame of the old press was rough-cut four-by-fours, whereas ours is made from commercial two-by-fours that hold top and bottom platforms of plywood. The old apple chopper was driven by a heavy flywheel powered by human arm strength, but ours is run by an electric motor spinning with a high-speed hum that would become irritating except that it is usually overwhelmed by the grinding rattle of disintegrating apples. The cylindrical bin that caught the chopped apple pieces in the 1920s was made of vertical wooden slats; in our lightweight model this slatted bin has been replaced by a 12-inch-long section of 8-inch white plastic pipe with holes drilled throughout its length. We still use arm strength to turn a threaded vertical shaft that pushes a plywood cap downward onto the apple pieces in the cylinder, just as they did in the old days. And gravity still works for us as it did in the 1920s, causing the sweet juice to stream off the bottom platform, through a narrow chute, and into a bucket. But the old-timey tin bucket has today been replaced with one made of plastic, a material that didn't exist nine decades ago. The enormous press in the photograph was moved into place and stayed there at least for the season, while ours is mobile, with a pair of lawn mower wheels under the front end and handles for pushing from the rear.

This freedom of movement is illusory, though, and limited to the length of my longest extension cord.

Every cider press, old or new, heavy or light, stationary or mobile, needs apples. We get ours from the Johnny Gunter orchard, even though there are plenty of apples around our home in Eugene. Johnny has been gone for many years, but his quirky, multivarietal orchard lives on and gives us the opportunity to inter-twine our lives with his, to carry his history in the Smith River valley into the future. Johnny's orchard has continuity with past generations as well; many of the varieties are the same as those in the old Gunter orchard where he grew up, ten miles further down Smith River. Johnny was an accomplished grafter, and he loved to tinker with his trees the way a mechanic would tinker with an engine. He spliced scions from several types of apples onto the limbs of existing trees, producing tailor-made mongrels, each bearing a unique mosaic of fruit. When Johnny's lifelong journey on Smith River finally ended, his orchard began to fall into decline. After twenty years of neglect I started pruning it back into shape, a years-long winter project of gradually lowering the towering treetops, removing branches that were damaged and diseased, opening the interior of the trees to sunlight, and training new growth to someday become fruit-bearing wood.

Despite my good intentions, the orchard is succumbing to age. The trees are older—not necessarily broken down and decrepit, just older. Disease is creeping into the trunks and branches, slowly killing them from the inside out. Yet every spring pink and white blossoms welcome the warm rain and intermittent sunshine, attracting pollinators of all kinds that spread the fertile yellow dust from flower to flower in an insect-mediated orgy of apple procreation. Every summer a new layer of sapwood grows hopefully over the dead places, while new suckers sprout like exuberant new hair. Every autumn the building crescendo of the apple year climaxes when the aging limbs put forth an abundance of fruit that could never have been anticipated in the bare-branched quiescence of winter.

An old Rome Beauty standing next to the orchard gate has apples so deeply red that they verge on purple. At least most of the tree is a Rome Beauty. Many years ago Johnny grafted a Red Delicious scion onto one of the lower limbs, and this autumn so many apples have ripened on the branch that part of it broke under the weight. Dad and I feel a little guilty that we didn't anticipate the collapse and prop up the limb, especially because this tree doesn't have a lot of fruit-bearing wood to spare. The year before when a cold wet spring severely reduced the pollination and there were almost no apples or fruit of any other kind in the Smith River valley, this Rome Beauty was one of the few trees to produce in the fall. A desperate bear was lured by the smell of ripening apples, dug under the orchard fence, and in the process of climbing and eating broke several of the large branches that I had been meticulously pruning back into shape. I wasn't happy about the damage, but who can fault a hungry bear?

No offense to bears, but my vision for the future of the orchard is considerably longer, and there are efficient methods for harvesting the apples that also preserve the tree and the hard won goals of my pruning. This usually involves someone climbing each tree and shaking the fruit down. That someone is always me. The main trunk of the Rome Beauty forks low to the ground into several smaller trunks, and I step easily upward, climbing the only way anyone can climb into an apple tree—one branch at a time. A downside of this shakedown strategy is that fallen apples are usually bruised. This isn't an issue for fruit that will shortly be blasted to smithereens in the cider press, but Mom and I like to save some of the best storage varieties for winter pies, and bruised apples rot. So I use the same trick I learned harvesting pears at the old Gunter orchard last September and begin by placing the largest, most pristine apples into the front of my tucked-in shirt. Then I swing out of the tree like a pregnant orangutan, find one of Johnny's handmade fruit boxes in the cinder-block root cellar, and squirrel the unblemished fruit away, safely out of sight of the cider pressers.

Hoisting myself back into the Rome, I quickly reach a place where the branches can be shaken hard enough to knock the apples loose. Dad stands well out of the way while I get in touch with my angry ape, bouncing up and down on limbs large enough to hold me, shaking and jerking all of them within my reach until my unleashed violence tears loose a torrent of falling apples that thrum to the ground like giant red hailstones. We gather them into a wheelbarrow with a rusty metal bin without a spot of paint left on it. But it is modern compared to the handmade, flatbed contraption in the antique cider pressing photograph. A wheelbarrow load of apples is heavy, and I put my legs into it for the trip down to the press.

By the time I roll in with the apples, Kim and the kids have arrived. Together with Mom they have set up a cider production line in front of the cabin. The progression from dirty apples to clean juice is not a trivial process. It starts with two galvanized washtubs filled with water from the garden hose and placed next to one another at the chopper end of the press. The first tub is a prewash that removes most of the grass, dead leaves, pieces of lichen, and bits of dirt clinging to the apples. This tub has been spiked with a glug of household bleach. We don't really like using bleach, but all of us love drinking fresh cider and don't want the experience marred by dose of *Escherichia coli*, a potentially nasty bacterium that could easily be transferred to the apples from deer or bear manure beneath the trees. The next tub contains only clean water, and is used to rinse off the bleach and any remaining detritus that might still be clinging to the apples. We don't take off the stems or cores or cull the fruit in any way, with the full understanding that untreated apples have worms and that the worms are still in there. We choose to believe that this enhances the overall flavor of the final product.

Kim takes the job of feeding apples into the funnel shaped hopper because she has the patience to put them through slowly enough that they don't jam up the chopper blades. I'm allowed to have this job only when no one else is available. Kim yells "Clear!" the signal that the chopper is about to be turned on and you damned well better have your hands out of the way. Then the electric motor hums and the blades whir and the first clean apples are dropped in. They aren't pulverized instantaneously. Instead the fruit bounces and rattles inside the hopper, shedding flesh in small pieces. A critical mass of apples is needed in the hopper—just enough so that their collective weight drives the fruit downward into the spinning blades but not so many that the chopper jams. But jams inevitably occur, and the incapacitated motor groans in protest. Someone switches off the motor, everyone shrugs, the hopper is removed, and the offending apple piece is fished out by hand. Then the hopper is replaced, someone yells "Clear!", the motor is restarted, and we fly back into action, relieved that this momentary constipation in our work flow has been dislodged.

After all the picking and other preparation, apple pieces are finally dropping from beneath the chopper into the cylinder below. The smell of cut apples wafts upward. Golden juice immediately begins dribbling out of the cylinder and down the bottom board, even without pressing, and Kim scrambles to place a bucket at the lower end to catch these first drops. Alex and Laurel, now fully alert and engaged, await the all important moment when the bin will be full of chopped apples and slid forward under the pressing mechanism. Pressing is the best job, and because they are kids they get to do it. They share the task of turning the crank, which screws the press downward onto the apple pieces, building the pressure that makes the juice gush from holes in the cylinder as though being forced from a fruit-filled artesian well. It streams through the narrow chute into the bucket, frothy foam floating to the surface like the head on a pitcher of draft ale.

All of the jobs at the press are covered, making Dad and me superfluous, so we take the wheelbarrow to the next apple tree. Although we don't know the names of most of the varieties in Johnny's orchard, over the years we have learned how each one tastes and figured out that the best cider comes from thoroughly mixing the sweet and tart fruit. There is nothing quantitative about this process, no weighing or measuring or tasting or test-ing for sugar content. We simply head for the next handy tree that has sweeter apples than the Romes we just picked, and this happens to be a Grimes Golden in the upper orchard. In years when some trees don't bear fruit, we don't have many choices. But this fall the apple gods have smiled and all of the trees are in full fruit. I climb and shake, and apples the color of light blackberry honey rain from the tree.

Apples are still rattling through the chopper when Dad and I return with the wheelbarrow full of Grimes Goldens. I upend the load onto the pile next to the press, and the fruit is immediately incorporated into the wash line. The pail that catches juice from the gushing cylinder is full, so we quickly switch it for an empty one. Then Mom holds a mesh bag over a larger five-gallon bucket while I pour the cider through to remove the wayward apple bits. When the cider-catching pail fills again with the sweet blond blood of Grimes Goldens, we filter this and mix it with the tart Rome juice.

Then it's time for the annual first tasting. Paper cups are passed around, dipped into the mixed juice, and tipped into waiting lips. I make my usual pronounce-ment: "Terrible as always!" We laugh at this bald-faced lie and get back to work. Proper cider mixing is proper living—you try a lot of different things without thinking too much about the process and trust that in the end it all works out.

Tree after tree, trip after trip with the rusty wheel-barrow, the apples accumulate by the press in a multi-colored heap. They glow in the late morning sun; soulful reds, flirtatious yellows, hopeful greens, and festive pink stripes. The mound expands outward from the center, its edges thinning onto the grassy lawn the way a baking cookie spreads across a pan in the heat of an oven. But the pile will grow no larger; the picking is finished.

After lunch our party mood becomes decidedly more chore-like. The apple mound gradually shrinks, and we are glad. Alex and Laurel realize that even the best job is still work, and they don't return to their post to squeeze the cider, so Dad and I trade off pressing. A horizontal piece of pipe that forms the crank on the press is now plastered with sticky apple juice that reacts chemically with the metal and stains my hands the color of prunes. My arms are tired from shaking trees and cranking the press. Yet I never get tired of watching that tannin-colored cider gush into the bucket at my feet.

All day, the pressed apple bits have been shaken out of the cylinder onto the compost heap thirty feet away. Tonight, after every trace of autumn sun has vanished and we have returned to 24-hour lighting in town, animals will come from the surrounding forest, slinking, waddling, lumbering, or stepping daintily through the darkness, drawn by the smell of a thousand crushed apples drifting out on gentle night breezes. I like to imagine raccoons, opossums, deer, and probably a bear forming a circle around the apple offal, feeding on it like nocturnal scavengers drawn to a carcass on an African savannah. In reality, they will come one or two at a time over many nights to gorge themselves on the brown mush, adding to their layer of fall fat. I wonder if they will overeat?

All of our large cider buckets are full, lined up in the shade of the porch, nearly thirty gallons of juice. Any reasonable person would stop. But I remain consumed by an obsessive, opportunistic drive to use the resource while it is available. Soon there will be no more daylight. Soon there will be no more autumn. Certainly there will be no more apples for nearly a year. Mom and Dad understand what drives me. Kim has learned to live with this behavior, and she tries to explain my passion to Alex and Laurel, who were ready to go home two hours ago. Years will pass before I know whether their mother has vindicated me. While the others chop and press the remaining apples, I frantically rummage through the cabin pulling together a peculiar collection of cider-worthy containers that can be filled and sealed shut for the ride home: a couple of quart canning jars, an insulated drinking water bottle, a half-gallon yogurt container with a snap-down lid. They are not enough for all of the juice remaining in the catch bucket. In desperation I grab the cooler that earlier held our lunch and pour in the last of the cider.

Back at home, I look intently into the old photograph and let my curiosity carry me deep below the surface of the image. The young men are happy. This lifts my spirits because I know that Johnny and Don did not have perfect childhoods. Their father was a product of his time, a taskmaster who used the rod excessively, and while no one can know for sure the true impact of those beatings, only one of the seven Gunter boys raised any children of his own. What is it about pressing cider that makes people happy, even people raised by a hard and determined man scratching out a subsistence living, people who went directly from youth into a life of logging and running sawmills, people who had to grow up too quickly?

Under my hard stare the image begins to soften and blur, but in my mind there is clarity. The photo becomes my family, smiling and busy around our cider press. I can see inside all of us, beyond all of the work and activity, see that we are happy. I smile because once a year we come together to receive what the land has given us. We don't think about work or school or newspaper headlines or unreal reality TV or real-life dramas. For one beautiful day we reach beyond our selfish idiosyncrasies and our traumas and team up as pickers, washers, choppers, pressers, strainers, fillers, and emptiers. One day seems like such a short time, a token really. Yet I wonder how many families are this blessed; to have a time when they gather on sacred ground, working with a unified purpose to produce something tangible, immediate, and delicious—all in just one beautiful fall day.

OCTOBER PARADOX

Days shorten relentlessly while
great fish with pumpkin flesh
surge upstream in a final race,
battered winners quietly dying
amid gaily colored leaves.

Gray dusk gathers the forest,
stretching the skin of my soul
so tightly that a ragged tear appears,
through which sighs a whisper of
infinite weariness.

Slipping into a silent pool,
gliding next to them,
frayed edges fluttering gracefully
in dim water,
I rest.

I don't like museums.

Confessions can be liberating, but this is a difficult admission, probably because I work at a university and am supposed to harbor a deep appreciation for all cultural and educational experiences. Mind you, I don't have anything *against* museums, and this fall I had the opportunity to see some of Europe's finest. But even the wonderful *Museo di Storia del Scienza* in Florence, where the great Galileo's mummified middle finger gestures defiantly toward the heavens, failed to resonate with me.

Honestly, I've tried to develop that deep awareness and emotional connection to art and history. But museums seem like lifeless places of observation compared with the overwhelming symphony of October life energy in the Pacific Northwest. Ancient conifers are awakened from their summer sonata of deep all-encompassing green by the brassy jazz solos of red, yellow, and orange hardwoods. Hormones well up in blacktail deer, apples ripen, and mushrooms pop to the surface, musky and glistening seductively in the subdued light of rapidly shortening days. Foragers with their fingers resting on the pulse of the land are consumed by an accelerating crescendo of picking, pickling, canning, and drying. October in my world is for full-on, unfettered living.

This furious drive to provision must come from a cellular knowledge, intercalated into our DNA over millions of Octobers, that winter is coming. October is a month of transition, the beginning of the rainy season, when painted leaves are torn from their branches and skitter about like lost souls wandering aimlessly in a netherworld between sap-filled summer and moldering winter. The exhilaration from the first storms gradually yields to the creeping reality that a long winter of short, gray days lies immediately ahead. October is schizophrenic, dangerous, stirring the emotions like no other month, and one never knows what might swirl to the surface. At times I would rather have been in hell than in October.

Nothing in my corner of the universe captures the paradox of October like Chinook salmon. After four years at sea, some combination of size and age conspire to overcome their ocean going transiency, those fat-filled days spent gorging on a swimming smorgasbord of herring, anchovies, and smelt. They return to freshwater using what seems to us a mysterious array of navigational tools. The glistening bounty of the open ocean is contained in those heavy silvery bodies, and their homecoming represents a massive influx of nutrients flowing into coastal watersheds that occurs with no human effort or intervention whatsoever. Following the storms of autumn, the ensuing gush of freshwater signals that all is ready in their natal streams. The fish then surge to the spawning gravels, consummate their lives in a frenzied fertility rite, and quietly die.

The coordinated return of all this potential food attracts a tremendous amount of attention. Seals, sea lions, and orcas nab adults in the estuaries, cutthroat trout scavenge loose eggs below the spawning fish, and crayfish feast on the decomposing dead. For indigenous peoples, salmon runs were the heart that sustained throbbing centers of society and commerce in lieu of nomadic hunting and gathering.

Now the world of salmon has changed. A self-regulating indigenous culture predicated on gratitude and the concept of "enough" has been replaced by a society driven by insatiable economic growth, one that uses dollars that have been derived either directly from salmon or from the ecosystems on which the fish depend. As a result, the runs have been overharvested, the oceans have become toxic dumping grounds, and spawning habitat has been blocked by dams or silted in by soils washed from clearcut hillsides. Native salmon runs are now being replaced by farm-raised caricatures, fattened in filthy, fenced-in pens and laced with a list of toxins only a chemist could pronounce.

Every fall the newspaper carries another article covering the decline of salmon. I can read those articles only in the bright light of the slanting October sun. Otherwise I risk falling into a black mood. My questions are always the same. How can we continue to think that everything is going swimmingly while the pulse of the salmon weakens? How can we stand by and watch the fish runs die from the vantage point of lives made materially comfortable by unsustainable extraction from the earth on which the salmon depend? How could we have partitioned our minds in a way that separates salmon well-being from human well-being?

If all this is progress, then today I intend to regress. In the predawn of Halloween morning I stand on a ridge lashed by a rain-filled demon howling out of the southwest. I'm an aspiring predator, and although my survival isn't predicated on eating salmon, I am compelled to become less civilized. A pitch-black opening into the forest is my point of departure, a trail away from all that is predictably organized, systematized, and categorized, a path disconnecting me from the comfortable museum of my everyday world and the loss of possibilities and freedom that have accompanied our shift from wild hunting-and-gathering humans to domesticated farm-raised workers penned in by the structures that define civilization. Periodically I need to leap that fence, swim free, and become an untethered animal.

The trail swallows me into the dark, dripping guts of the forest. Wind gusts pound the opposite side of the ridge on my left, then pour over the top, knocking showers of water from an archway of spruce branches above me. My headlamp creates a small bubble of artificial light, a diver's helmet in a sea of blackness. Soaking wet salal and sword fern brush my legs, and within minutes my pants are soaked. My neoprene chest waders remain rolled in my backpack, dry and useless.

Deep into the canyon, the familiar roar from an unseen creek reaches upward out of the darkness. Then gray daylight slowly begins to penetrate the ancient forest, allowing me to ditch the headlamp. My old running shoes lose traction in slippery mud, and in the abject solitude amorphous fears coalesce into conscious thoughts. If I broke my leg, how long would I lie here? Where's the resident cougar napping this morning? Somewhere in my center, just below the ribs, a space begins to form. That feeling. A cell phone in my pocket would only deprive me of this loneliness.

Arriving at the bottom of the canyon, still alone and limbs intact, I shed my pack under a large red cedar with boughs impervious to the incessant rain. The creek is running low and clear, still placid after five previously rainless days. A small sandbar from which I usually fish is exposed. On the opposite side, Old Dead Alder has finally toppled, her feet on the bank, body stretching into the water, skeletal arms reaching skyward, while gentle currents eddy around her, nibbling at her crumbling flesh.

The salmon are here. They are always here after the rains begin. Occasionally one swirls at the surface of the long slow pool in front of me, while others splash noisily as they negotiate a shallow riffle above the hole. They are in various stages of dissolution. Two fish spawn in the current ten feet away, dark bodies highlighted against sandy, freshly churned gravel. Others languish in quiet water, nearly lifeless, tattered tail fins undulating like small white prayer flags in a soft breeze. The dead are where happenstance has deposited them, lying gracefully on the bottom or hung awkwardly from a submerged branch. A Picasso stirs passion in some. But this is my canvas; I am consumed by a primordial impulse to wade in and participate in this uncensored, unvarnished drama, to become a part of the whole wallowing, thrashing, breeding, dying mess.

Soon my line is drifting through the head of the pool. Every year hooking the first salmon is a shock, but they always behave similarly. When the hook sets, the fish makes a brief run to the top of the hole, then swaps directions, torpedoing past me toward the lower end. The line draws tight, and raw power on the other end instantly travels through the rod and into my arms, resulting in surging adrenal glands and a screaming reel. Animal instinct prevails as I become physically connected to this fish, reacting to each twist and turn and shake of the head.

Halfway to the bottom of the pool the huge fish reverses course and heads back upstream. A silvery flash and rounded snout confirm that this is a hen, rather than a hook-jawed buck, fresh from the bay six miles down. The stakes are immediately raised because I now have every intention of eating her. Spawning salmon darken over time, an inevitable decay process initiated by their return to freshwater. Dark fish usually taste terrible and are best released to finish the business of spawning, having been interrupted by the painful indignation of being yarded around on the end of a line. But this nickel-bright hen is now fighting for her life.

I'm battling for mine, too. Although an industrialized food chain has robbed me of the privilege of starving if I don't land this fish, eating a wild salmon caught in a wild place feeds some untamed corner of my soul, a space I guard jealously from the insidious intrusions of modern living. There was a time when I failed to nurture this part of me, and I became a museum piece, hard as stone, a lifeless relic of my past. This darkening of my spirit finally came to a head in the dimming days of an October past, when I was bailed out temporarily by the wonders of pharmacology; better living through biochemistry. Now I go fishing.

The salmon makes surge after relentless surge, but these eventually shorten. Total focus dissolves time so I have no idea how long this has gone on, but a dull ache pervades my arms and shoulders. Because I am alone, the fish must be negotiated to within reach of a short gaff no longer than my forearm. She moves into a space between the bank and me, precariously close to some brush at water's edge, just out of reach. Succumbing to momentary panic, I try to strong-arm her away from the submerged branches. She is so close that my rod is bent completely double and only six feet of line is out. All the elasticity in my underweight system, a technological wonder wrought of stretchable nylon and flexible fiberglass, is gone. Physics bites me on the butt. The line snaps, recoiling back through the rod guides to dangle in flaccid futility.

For perhaps two seconds the exhausted salmon lies next to the bank, unaware that with one swish of her great tail she could swim free. But the first move is mine. I lunge toward her, plunging my left arm with the gaff down and forward into the cold water. In an instant I'm stumbling out of the creek, dragging the heavy fish up a steep bank. A strategic whack with the gaff handle, the finality of quivering fins, a crazy, mixed-up flood of exaltation and excitement, sadness and sorrow, satisfaction and remorse, and it is over.

But not really. There is beauty in landing a large fish to eat. Catching it is only a beginning. Floating the hen back to the sandbar, I carefully remove gills and guts, hiding them in a place only the raccoons and crayfish will find. Two skeins of swollen eggs the color of ripe persimmons, perhaps five pounds in all, go in a plastic bag to be cured for caviar. At home, the carcass will be filleted, some eaten fresh, some smoked, some canned and consumed over winter. Head, fins, and skeleton will be boiled for soup stock, and the cooked bones will become calcium in my garden compost.

Nothing is wasted out of respect for the salmon and all that she has lived. Yet my connection to her is much more. I want to wake up every day with the raw, pervasive certainty that I am everything that is this fish. I want to capture the surge of her carbon and calcium in my bones and muscles and the vibration of her hydrogen and nitrogen in the coiled memory of my chromosomes. I want my entire being to slash through schools of smelt, struggle upstream past orange crayfish, spawn a new generation in colorful gravel, then slip into a quiet eddy and rest in the sureness of my own death. I want the fundamental understanding that this fish is only on loan to me, that my existence is a loan from the Universe, and that despite our cozy partitions around space and time, our artificial withins and withouts, beginnings and endings, the reality of our place is temporal and spatial unity. Therein lies the resolution of the paradox that is October. It is an illusion.

The cycle of my day continues. I hook several more fish but land none. My casting arm aches. Rain beats steadily down, occasionally propelled horizontally by gusts of wind hurtling up the canyon. The creek rises. Leaden daylight fades almost imperceptibly, and the oncoming dusk is acknowledged by something deep within my diurnal core. A lonely wordless weariness of spirit reaches up from some nameless abyss, encircling my heart with cold, wet fingers. At first I struggle, then give myself over to it, allowing the feeling to become fully formed. Inhaling deeply, I reach inside, stroking the thing gently, and then exhale. The wraith releases me from its grasp, riding out on my breath and swirling downstream with green alder leaves, out to sea. Another paradox resolved.

Packing up, I shoulder my load and begin the long slog upward.

CHANTERELLE FOREST

I have changed.

In a small moment in a small living room at a small November gathering of friends I realized that I was now a different person, that over time I had been transformed in the way that darkness and shadow slowly expand through autumn.

It happened when someone said, "Hey, chanterelles are $6.95 a pound at the Market!" I was polite and tried to validate their enthusiasm with "Wow!" But for me that innocuous proclamation had stirred up an internal puff of silt that temporarily muddied an otherwise clear flow of congenial conversation. In that instant I understood that I can no more go to the grocery store and buy chanterelles than a whale can take up walking. A part of my brain that would have once allowed me to trade money directly for a bag of mushrooms had either atrophied to the point of incapacity or been transformed into something entirely new.

Just as biologists who study the history of life on the planet withhold judgment on the changes they observe in nature, I don't view my altered outlook toward fungi as superior. In fact, a strong case could be made that my compulsion to forage is maladaptive. Getting mushrooms now requires that I set aside a large part of one fall weekend day when I should be raking leaves, cleaning gutters, mowing the lawn one last time, winterizing the mothballed lawnmower, de-mossing the roof, pruning the laurel hedge, storing empty fruit boxes, and godknows how many other prewinter projects. After ignoring all of these responsibilities, I get in the pickup and burn some of my children's fossil fuel inheritance to drive a twisting road deep into the Coast Range and wander aimlessly through wet underbrush. All of this could be avoided were I to spend ten bucks and ten minutes of my time buying chanterelles at the market.

Yet living efficiently is no longer my goal. Chanterelles grow in the forest, where the energy of life flows in complex ways that can't be measured in arbitrary units of time and money. In November the land has been bathed by the first rains of autumn, washing over yellowing hardwoods, dripping from green conifers, carrying away the dust kicked up in the exuberance of summer, carrying away the birdsong. The forest is silent—mostly. But if you are very still, if you listen with your entire body in the spaces between heartbeats, you can feel the faint rustle of fungi pushing upward through damp duff, feel the swell of moss cells plumping with water, feel the swirl of a spawning Coho's tail, feel the rhythmic rush of wind over the beating wings of a raven. In the quiet instant between breaths you can feel the moisture opening the pores of your skin, until you are drinking in the forest. Then you are no longer just you.

In the quiet places and silent spaces where chanterelles live, we can breach the boundaries of self, experience a level of personal dissolution that becomes the knowledge of connectedness among all things. The partitions permeating our lives begin to fall away—

economy, environment, religion, politics, nature, nurture, state, country, minute, hour, mine, yours, us, them—and can be seen for what they really are: arbitrary constructs that help us to make sense of, talk about, and divide up our anthropocentric universe. These human ideas about how the world works do not necessarily translate into reality. In the *real* world, the one with fungi emerging from living soil dampened by rain that rose from a tropical ocean thousands of miles away to fall on trees green with chlorophyll using light energy from a star 93,000,000 miles distant to make the oxygen that we breath while walking about in search of chanterelles, those divisions are meaningless.

So yes, I have changed. I must now pick my own mushrooms.

Fourteen hours of November darkness have given way to a rare sunny morning. Light pours through the large front window of the Johnny Gunter cabin, filling the room, driving away the last of my sleep. When the weather turns cold I sleep on the long comfortable couch in the front room, bringing me closer to the heat from the woodstove. The house is drafty and uninsulated, and sleeping here also allows me to keep the stove burning during long, cold nights. Apparently I have slept soundly for several hours, because morning is now fully formed and the stove is a chilly corpse across the room. I crawl from my warm nest of rumpled blankets into the cold room, pull on cold pants, light the cold stove, and in a few minutes the firebox returns to life, drawing low-throated, pulsing breaths through the front vents that could be the throbbing climax of a grouse drum. Light energy stored for decades within the wood is quickly converted into hot orange flames that push the cold back out through loose windowpanes.

The confluence of events that brought me here this morning began as a collection of rivulets that form after a long, steady rain and at first appear to have nothing in common with one another except that all are running down the same hill. Earlier in the month I bagged a deer. A week later I was picking chanterelles with friends when we ran into an obnoxiously extroverted forager who said that dried, pulverized chanterelles are really good on steaks. I didn't like the guy, but I had a freezer full of venison that might benefit from a good drubbing in dried mushrooms. My stash of dehydrated delectables collected earlier in the fall was small and would be enough to season only a couple of venison dinners. When someone put my share of the day's chanterelles in a plastic rather than a paper bag and they rotted before I could dry them, I found myself in an unusual pickle; this winter my mushrooms would run out well before my supply of venison.

To rectify this imbalance in my personal universe, I leave the warm house behind. Fortified with instant coffee, instant oatmeal, and powerful resolve, I climb the gentle slope of the frosty meadow, wading through brown, knee-high bracken fern and grass, a dusting of ice crystals collecting like powdered sugar on the cuffs of my wool pants. Big trees loom like friendly giants across the upper side of the meadow. A trail slips into the shadowy embrace of the old forest, where a steady succession of rains has soaked through the dense overstory. The matronly arms of the huge trees embrace the accumulated moisture, and the cold damp air holds the fragrance of decomposing wood, the mildewy body odor of a host of microbial minions feeding on shed needles, limbs, and fallen trees, hastening the return of wood to the soil. Shafts of morning sunlight stab through the fog-shrouded canopy, angular beams intersecting dark perpendicular trunks.

Within a hundred yards I arrive at a perennial spring that is the water source for the cabin. A dozen golden chanterelles have sprouted from thick green moss near the springhouse. They are an odd excuse for a mushroom. Most are misshapen funnels that seem to have been irrevocably contorted by being birthed from soft darkness beneath the forest floor into the unpredictable roller coaster of autumn life above ground. They are orange, but not crazy, vivid, hurt-your-brain orange. Chanterelles are the color of wild salmon flesh, the color of vine maple leaves that graduated from yellow but chose not to pursue red, the color of a low hanging autumn sun setting through thin overcast. The orange glow of chanterelles is the purposeful energy of living things that know the boundaries of life, things that understand that their time is limited and that certain tasks must be accomplished. My time is limited also—my day, my autumn, my life—and on this morning that is very near the end of chanterelle season, my task is to pick enough mushrooms to last the winter. This is my perception for the moment.

At their most basic level, chanterelles are good food. Their color is the radiant energy of beta-carotenes, the same pigment found in carrots and squash. Beta-carotenes are antioxidants, a pack of chemical predators that course through our system hunting down free radicals that contribute to all kinds of problems from cancer to heart disease to aging. We cannot make our own beta-carotenes; they must be consumed. And while I'm happy to grow pampered domesticated vegetables, I'm happier yet to kneel on the prayer mat of moist moss and with a small knife trim the chanterelles at ground level, dropping them into a cloth shopping bag.

Turning off the trail, I move more deeply into the forest, more deeply into my mind. Something furtive is lurking in the shadowy draws that furrow my cerebral cortex, and I pretend not to look. The chanterelles are engaging enough. They are everywhere. This year the fungal frenzy erupting from the forest floor is nearly inconceivable, even to long-time foragers. My mycologist friends tell me that because our rainy season began at the end of summer, the warm, damp weather stimulated an inordinate amount of growth. A fungus is mostly a well-kept secret of underground strands called mycelia that occasionally put up fruiting bodies, the things that we recognize as mushrooms. These are the fungal version of sex, and while I can't really speak for them, there doesn't appear to be anything particularly recreational or bonding about it. Mushrooms are simply a way for fungi to reshuffle the genetic deck and throw off a host of spores that will germinate into a new mycelial mass. That they are good for you and are great on venison seems to be a happy biological accident.

My bag begins to fill quickly, and I move westward along a bench that long ago was the streambed of Upper Smith River now meandering across the valley floor 100 feet below me. I hurry for no reason, rushing across this bench that might have been half a million years in the making, hurrying past trees seven feet in diameter that have been here for two hundred years. The hum of a hurrying car reaches into the forest, a reminder that this stand is a mere fragment of its former self. People hurried to take down big trees like these, hurried to feed the timber boom that was the economic bread and butter of this region for the majority of the previous century, hurried to make "progress" by subjugating the forests to the demands of a civilization based on the physical impossibility of endless growth.

Despite the ecological absurdity of this economic paradigm, I have been sullied by it—I am hurrying to pick chanterelles. An old forest should inspire leisurely, quiet reverence, but I crash recklessly forward through knee-deep salal with no respect for the sanctuary within which I am now a participant. Abruptly I push out of the underbrush into a small opening with a mossy floor and some young well-spaced hemlock trees. Stepping quietly across the thick green carpet, stopping to trim off more mushrooms, the envelope of silence seems to intensify my internal chatter. I become aware that my loud bushwhacking is a reflection of the rattling inside my own head. My eyes scan the forest floor for mushrooms while my mind flies from one thought to the next—lab work at the university, late fall fixit chores, lost political causes, Laurel's birthday slumber party, and lyrics from the Dave Mathews Band: "I am, who I am, who I am…"

Who am I? If I really am my thoughts, then right now things seem pretty damned complicated. Emotions swirl like dark water in the wake of my unhinged, off-track, out-of-control thoughts. If I were in grade school I'd be medicated for attention deficit disorder. From somewhere within this cacophony of neural noise, I begin to wonder how long I would need to wander in the forest before the internal din subsided. Moses needed forty years and Jesus forty days, but they didn't have to keep track of their vacation time.

That thing lurking around the edges of my morning now steps fully and deliberately into the open. I realize that I am angry. Not just pee-ohhed. Angry to the basement bottom of my soul. I am angry for every road-scarred clearcut and for every baby Coho choked on silt and every gallon of herbicide ever sprayed and for every two-by-four I ever bought; angry for every dam that blocked a river and every salmon that would never die at home and for every kilowatt of hydropower I ever used; angry for the rock mined from river bottoms and every mile of every road I ever drove on that gravel; angry for no-taste, no-name, no-story, no-soul petrochemical food and every plastic package of it I ever ate; angry for smoggy skies obscuring the gold-smattered hills of autumn and for every piece of wood I ever burned to heat my house; angry for economics and economists and every living thing that has died in the name of a sound economic decision and for my own retirement account; angry for every politician and every corporate lobbyist who paid them to doom the biosphere to a long, slow death and for every time I was suckered into voting for them; angry for every person sitting on every street corner begging for my money and for every time I turned my back; angry that I am picking mushrooms in this peaceful forest, standing here in my anger and thinking that if I were to focus all this angry energy it would cause me to self-combust and I would be immolated in a pillar of chanterelle-orange flame.

But anger is the eruption on the surface, a secondary emotion caused by something molten deep within. I become still and begin to follow the path of my breathing inward, allowing this little grove of old growth to fuel my imagination, carrying me back a thousand years, before all the logging and road building and planting and herbicides and thinning that now collectively pass for "intensive forest management," returning to a time when old forests dominated the land, embracing it in an enduring state of ecological climax, a time when salmon and spotted owls and salamanders were never in the news, when "tree sitting" was a rest stop for undomesticated humans who traveled the dim vastness.

I return to a time before the feeling or the concept or the word *anger*. And I realize that then there was no anger because there was no emotional wounding from human-induced ecocide. That was a time before people scurried over the earth separated from the biosphere by layers of civilized complexity designed to make their lives easier, "better." That was before humans had locked themselves in a silent, windowless, padded cell of modern living, shielded from the trauma of watching the living world die as a result of adding more insulation to their cubicle.

We are wounded even in our isolation. Millions of years of evolution have etched into our chromosomes a need for deep connections to the land and other people that is as immutable as the rocks that have become our bones that carry us around in this green world. In *A Sand County Almanac*, Aldo Leopold framed our evolutionary relationship to the biosphere in moral terms. He understood that we function as moral humans only when we act upon our empathic connectedness to one another, and he challenged us to expand this concept of morality to become a moral species making moral choices with respect to both our fellow humans *and* our place in the community of the Earth. This requires us to become fundamentally connected to our bioregion as well as to our fellow humans. The alternative—to remain within our self-constructed, self-imposed cell, trapped in entitlement, parasitizing and ultimately killing our ecological life support—is to become biologically and morally destitute.

So we arrive at a profound and tragic paradox. We must throw open the windows, break out of our cubicle, trade recycled air for oxygen made by real trees, give up hard black asphalt for delicate green moss, dump the vitamin pills, and forage for wild mushrooms. We must travel further along the path toward intimacy with the land. But in doing these things we will be hurt. We will be traumatized.

Despite this risk, I choose the path of reconciliation. I accept that I will be damaged. But I will not be destroyed by my wounded anger. Instead I will forgive. I forgive because I must; because if I don't then upon my reentry into the atmosphere of the living world I will be obliterated in the fire of my own resentment. Instead, I choose twisted vine maple and forgiveness, slanting autumn sun and shadows on sword fern and forgiveness, a gentle trickle of spring water over sandstone and forgiveness, a young hemlock tree growing from a sawed-off stump and forgiveness, the soft silence of an owl's feathers and cool salamander skin and the tiny hot breath of a winter wren chattering in the salal and forgiveness. I choose to forgive self-centered human blundering and insensitivity, especially my own, even though I do not forgive easily. I choose my wife and children and friends and forgiveness. I choose to watch the landscape heal. I choose to heal myself.

Change is hard, and old habits seem immortal. I am mortal. Achieving a lasting level of attentive emotional control will require time, training, and certainly more chanterelle hunting.

Closing my eyes, I continue to take more diaphragmatic breaths, listening intently to the hush of the autumn afternoon, imagining the word slooww-lyyy in two clear syllables. The forest breathes with its own rhythm, its own breath, its own mindfulness, a silent resonance that patiently soothes my overheated, recalcitrant neurons. My pulse drops, and I am enveloped in the coolness of evaporating sweat.

My mushroom bag isn't quite full, but I'm tired of lugging it around. The feeling of tension deep within my chest, the foraging mojo that has been driving me since morning, slowly fades with the aging afternoon. My chanterelle shortage has been resolved for another year, although the healing of my spirit will be a lifetime project. Turning downhill, I ease between vine maple trunks, slip between clumps of sword fern, circle around dense patches of salal, slooww-lyyy, quietly letting the gentle arms of gravity draw me toward the sunlit meadow, back to the cabin.

I will change.

LAST DANCE

There will be no more chanterelles this year. A glorious fall that saved my late-blooming tomatoes and winter squash came to an abrupt end early in December with a week-long Arctic chill that froze everything solid, including some of my pipes. Then came the next rainstorm, quickly melting the few lingering mushrooms back into the duff from which they came. Frozen petioles of thimbleberry and salmonberry thawed, and the last yellow leaves returned quietly to the earth.

My garden in town has been put to bed for the winter, tucked under a layer of newspaper and cardboard to keep down the weeds. Only the cold hardy vegetables remain, collards with leaves like green canoe paddles, serrated wild kales bred on Siberian steppes. The plants will receive no more attention beyond periodic harvesting of their nutrient-rich leaves. Meticulously collected vegetable seeds—lettuce, corn, dry beans, tomatoes, and squash—are packed away, each with an embryonic plant lying curled within a nutritive layer of endosperm, waiting for a new garden with renewed soil, waiting for the light. My year is recorded on the pantry shelves: potatoes, winter squash, and jars of blackberry jam, peaches, pears, apple cider, clams, and salmon. The cold snap has induced a pervasive sense of dormancy that I find a relief after the manic days of summer and fall. Following nine months of constant motion and outwardly pouring energy I turn inward to rest, reflect, recharge.

In these days culminating in the Winter Solstice, daylight goes through one final retrenchment. While this amounts to only a small change in available daylight, the transfer of those few minutes of light into growing darkness is like childbirth, where the final contractions require an extraordinary amount of energy. My spirit contracts also, as though I'm closing off the now empty rooms of a once full house. Curling up, I retreat into the endosperm of my living room, bank my internal fire to maintain a bed of coals that can be fanned back to life by the lengthening days of February. This woodstove approach to overwintering can be tricky; care must be taken to avoid shutting things down too far and risk killing the coals. My fire has died before.

This morning my coals need a bit of fanning. Because I don't have either the inclination or the resources for a quick flight to a sun-parched winter retreat like Cabo or New Zealand, I settle instead for a year-end drive to Smith River. The back route is now burned into my synapses, inscribed on my being, as though I could close my eyes and will the pickup along the entire route. There is no contempt in this familiarity; every trip is slightly different, a registry of the changing seasons and vicissitudes of weather. As of this morning the temperature in the hills above 1,000 feet hasn't risen above freezing for three days, and fog has accreted into a crystalline hoar frost on the evergreens, covering them in druidic white cloaks that blur the boundary between forested hillsides and sun-broken vapors, a quantum perspective on the landscape.

Midday is approaching when I pull into the Gatchell place. Jerry is on front the porch splitting kindling for the wood cook stove, his yard-long braid coiled discreetly beneath a red beret. He's been out and about already today; the front of his canvas chaps are wet.

We exchange the usual "hi-how-ya-doin?"

"Do you have time to show me those fish?"

Jerry pushes the far horizon of the concept "laid back," and if he's ever been upset or in a hurry I haven't been party to it. For him "now" is almost always a good time. He disappears inside for his binoculars and digital camera while I wait outside. The late December sun barely clears a ragged line of Douglas firs topping the south ridge and casts a patch of wan, fish-belly light next to a deceased Volkswagen Beetle, its white paint slowly giving way to creases of green moss, a real life rendition of the cave-dwelling car in the movie *Sleeper*. I wander into this small warm place and squint gratefully into the weak sunshine.

Jerry returns with his shoulder bag for the trip to Bear Creek. Parking at the pavement, we hike leisurely up a gravel road that follows the creek then turn right into dark brush. The lower reaches of the small stream wind through elderly Douglas fir, western red cedar, gray-green trunks of vine maple, brown salmonberry canes, and stiff evergreen leaves of salal. In the womb of the forest, the pre-Solstice sun filters through only in occasional patches, lighting a mossy trunk here, a patch of salal there.

Bear Creek is one of Jerry's special places, and he knows what he is about here. His path is a wandering but efficient means of moving along the brushy canyon bottom, skirting the densest salmonberry thickets and largest downed logs. He recites the history of each fallen tree as though he were recounting the funerals of dead relatives—this one 20 years ago, that one 3 years ago, another a convenient bridge across the creek before being covered by the relentlessly growing underbrush. We use the more recent casualties as causeways above the thickest of the thickets. The small creek murmurs insistently as we draw closer, always polite, never overbearing, an earthbound call to afternoon prayers. We are strolling through a 200-year-old cathedral.

We push carefully through the brush next to the creek. Flotsam along the edges of the channel indicates that last week's rains drove the placid brook into a short-lived snit. But the water has calmed itself and today is running nearly clear, retaining only the milky hue of sun-baked glass. Deposited inside each bend is a miniature beach of fresh, untracked sand, its pristine nakedness nearly begging for new footprints of raccoon, mink, and otter. The sandbars are the bones of the mountains that have been relentlessly ground by water and are now beginning their long path to the Pacific where they will spend future millennia as dunes shifting restlessly around the mouth of the Umpqua River.

These are the tiny streams into which Coho salmon are compelled to return and spawn. When autumn rains break the summer drought, sending drifts of alder leaves into coastal rivers, the fish begin their way back to Bear Creek. They use their sense of smell to winnow this creek from seemingly limitless other possibilities, detecting subtle differences in water chemistry, sniffing out that unique signature, that perfect match to the template that was somehow stamped into their brains in the weeks after hatching. Smells can be this way, probing and poking at the cracks in our exterior shell until they find their way into that deep inner place, drawing us home.

The gentle burble of the creek is overpowered by violent splashing. Jerry and I stay put, waiting for the arrival of the fish, but the splashing continues from the same spot, out of sight around a bend. We step forward through a densely packed group of old conifers, growing so closely together that their shoulders nearly touch, slide between vine maple trunks, carefully approaching the creek like latecomers slipping unobtrusively into a service already in progress.

Below us is a female Coho, her 30-inch body incongruously large in this thin filament of water. She is three years old, ripe with eggs, and beat up by the 60-mile river trip from Umpqua Bay. Her tattered white tail gently fans the soft current, expending just enough energy to keep her body stationary. Her dorsal fin is also white and shredded, bony fin rays protruding like thin skeletal fingers from her darkly speckled back. Tipping on her side, she thrashes violently against golden sandstone pebbles, churning the water into silty froth, probing the gravel for that single sweet spot into which she will dig out a redd and deposit her eggs. In the shallows her upturned flank flashes with the colors of a dying winter sunset.

From our vantage point behind a clump of damp sword ferns above the creek we spot her potential mate, a buck swimming into view just downstream. His nuptial physique is outrageous; elephantine nose hooking grotesquely downward, humped back culminating in a ragged white ridge, flanks a gaudy holly berry red. He reminds me of a used up Travolta-like dandy from a 1970's discotheque.

But the hen's opinion is the only one that matters, and she seems to appreciate his ridiculous attire. She splashes upstream through an especially narrow, gravelly chute into the next pool, again listing onto her side, thrashing the gravel. Resting briefly, she returns downstream, back to the buck in the pool eight feet below. They lie quietly, side by side. Leaning slightly, the buck applies a shuddering stroke to her left flank. The contact seems to restrain her and she remains there for a few minutes before flopping over for another churning trip into the upstream pool. This time the buck joins her, pulling alongside, nudging against her rose-colored side, apparently realizing somewhere in the depths of his piscine brain that he must follow her lead and that subtle persistence is the only way. Humans should be so perceptive.

The circling dance of the Coho continues, while Jerry and I remain quiet observers. Not everyone in the forest shares our disengagement; river otter tracks in the fresh sand attest to the danger these fish encounter in the final days of their journey. I hope the otter will wait until the salmon have finished their final task, wait until the redd is covered and fertile eggs are nestled in sandstone pebbles awaiting their life, wait until the parents are quietly waiting on death, awaiting the otter. I have no say in this matter, nor will I take issue with predatory opportunism. The otter and I have held common ground.

The ritual ballet in the stream below could continue for days before culminating in a final outburst of reproductive energy that will produce the fertile eggs of another generation. Over many more days the fish will quietly die, and weeks will pass as they dissolve back into the circulating lifeblood of this place. By that time I will be harvesting the nettles emerging from the moist, sandy canyon bottoms, plants full of carbon, nitrogen, and phosphorous that was transported from the ocean by fish long dead, and tiny salmon fry will be waiting their turn in the flowing water of the nursery gravel.

While I would very much love to see the salmon through to their nuptial consummation, I simply don't share their endurance. For now I am happy that they have fed my sun-deprived spirit, happy that they have shown me the joy in circles. Salmon circles are more than two-dimensional lines, more than my life traced on a map from Oregon to Kansas to New York to St. Louis and back. Salmon circles are living and hyper-dimensional. They are a spawning creek flowing through canyons with fast riffles and slow pools of time stream-ing through shifting light and color and smells and fork-ing channels with mistakes and not learning and the same mistakes with learning and different mistakes all done with senses open to some vague notion of progress and an end that isn't really. Then when the extraordinary circular ride closes on itself, we hope for wisdom.

Oh, do I hope for wisdom. Once I thought of time as spooling into the infinite future like some never end-ing kite string. In the days when I was swimming and growing far out at sea, struggling through school, thrash-ing out a career that would bring me no closer to home, I ventured too close to the precipice of infinity, teetered, then caught my balance. I swore never to go near that edge again. Now I swim in a clear water world of big fish dancing and dying in small streams, feeding ancient trees that become rotting logs that become more trees, sandstone mountains that turn into nesting gravels that become sandbars that wash out to sea that are pressed into new rocks that make new mountains—a world where time runs in ceaseless, interconnected, multidimensional cycles.

Six in the evening and the late January sky is lit with a hopeful trace of gray sunset. The Coho eggs have hatched by now. Leaving work, I bicycle south across town into the near darkness, cool air coursing across my cheeks while high over my left shoulder a three-quarter moon burns with cool intensity through broken clouds. A din of chorus frogs becomes audible from a shallow pond ten blocks farther south. Their mass trilling grows in intensity on my right as I pedal toward them, reaching its crescendo when I cross busy Hilyard Street. Turning away from the pond, I pass the troll-like shadows of willow clumps along Amazon Creek, as the frog chorus recedes quickly into the night behind. Naked limbs of Oregon ash are backlit by halogen streetlights and the self-absorbed evening traffic along Hilyard. Homeless people talk loudly from the blackness near the creek while a killdeer circles above, crying repeatedly and invisibly in the night, perhaps also wondering where it will sleep. Turning onto my own street, a neighbor calls out a greeting from her unlit porch. A familiar bump marks the entry into our driveway; the garage door sticks from winter humidity. Then a warm house, my wife, the aroma of dinner.

I am home.

Made in the USA
Middletown, DE
18 February 2021